FOREWORD

According to an unknown source, 'architecture is man's greatest endeavour'. If there is substance to this, then all buildings are infinitely intriguing objects of beauty, symbols of their age, and emblems of human wisdom and creativity.

Straiton (St. Cuthbert's) Parish Church, the subject of this book, is a building rich in history and architectural refinement. In the chapters that follow, the author skilfully navigates the reader through already charted, and uncharted waters of its amazing history, while at the same time describing in detail its stunning decor – which have led to this sanctuary's status as 'a gem in Ayrshire's architectural crown'.

The author has also placed the development of the church within the wider context of Scottish ecclesiastical and political history, and in relation to the growth of Straiton village and its institutions.

James Kirk deserves our deepest gratitude for undertaking this project, for the exhaustive research which has brought it to fruition, and for collating a mass of material into manageable proportion and accessible form. Our warmest appreciation is also accorded to Stenlake Publishing, Catrine, Ayrshire, for their sterling service in making a manuscript available in print to an enquiring public.

Although Straiton Kirk is of outstanding historical and architectural significance, it is our prayer that the reader will appreciate its primary purpose as a place of pilgrimage and Christian worship; and that over-arching all the centuries of its existence there is the unfailing providence of Almighty God – to whom be praise and thanksgiving, now and for ever.

May those who worship here be faithful to the vision of our fathers in the Faith, who have bequeathed to us this unique inheritance, and long preserve this church as a prime spiritual resource and 'a house of prayer for all nations.'

W. Gerald Jones
Minister at Straiton
August 2019

PAISLEY ABBEY

Paisley Abbey was founded when Walter Fitzalan, the High Steward of Scotland (whose descendants became the House of Stewart/Stuart) signed a charter for the priory to be set up in land he owned in Paisley in 1163. It is believed that Saint Mirin (or Saint Mirren) founded a community on this site in the 7th century. Sometime after his death a shrine to him was established which became a popular site of pilgrimage. Set up on the site of an old Celtic church by thirteen monks, the priory was raised to the status of an Abbey in 1245 and was dedicated to four saints; St. Mary, St. James, St. Milburga and St. Mirin, who had brought Christianity to the church site in the 6th century. The Abbey held patronage over St. Cuthbert's of Stratoun until 1236 when it was passed to Crossraguel which had been erected as a condition of the earlier grant to Paisley.

The modern Abbey dates from the 12th century, based on a former Cluniac monastery. Following the Reformation in the 16th century, it became a Church of Scotland parish kirk. The name Paisley may derive from the Brythonic (old Welsh) *Passeleg*, 'basilica' (derived from the Greek), meaning 'major church', recalling an early, though undocumented, ecclesiastical settlement.

The Abbey went on to be wealthy and influential under royal patronage, with extensive trade between the Paisley location and commercial centres in Europe. Paisley Abbey would also become a centre for learning. Sir William Wallace, a key figure in the Wars of Scottish Independence in the 13th century, is believed to have been educated by the monks of Paisley Abbey. Much of the original building was burned down in 1307, but it was rebuilt later in the 14th century.

In 1315 Walter Stewart, the 6th High Steward of Scotland, married Marjory Bruce, the daughter of the Scottish king Robert the Bruce. The following year, a heavily pregnant Marjory fell while out horse riding near Paisley Abbey. She was taken to the Abbey infirmary where she died, but her unborn child was saved after a caesarean delivery and would become King Robert II of Scotland, the first of the Stewart monarchs. This led the Abbey to claim itself as the 'cradle of the Royal House of Stewart.' The Stewarts, one of the most enduring royal dynasties in Scottish history – began with Robert II taking the throne as King of Scots in 1371. The Abbey is also the final resting place of six High Stewards of Scotland, Princess Marjory Bruce, and the wives of King Robert II and King Robert III.

In 1491 absolution was granted by Abbot George Shaw, representing the Pope and in the presence of the relics, to James IV of Scotland and others implicated in the death of James III at the Battle of Sauchieburn.

By 1499 Shaw had built a new, larger pilgrims' chapel and added the sculptured stone frieze which can still be seen today, showing scenes from the life of St. Mirin. It was originally brightly painted and may have been part of a rear panel of an altar before being put up as a frieze on the wall.

CROSSRAGUEL
Foundation of the Abbey (1200–1268)

Patronage of St. Cuthbert of Straiton was vested in Crossraguel conditional on a Cluniac Abbey being established there by the monks at Paisley.

The golden age of Scottish ecclesiastical architecture, inaugurated by David the First, the "sair sanct for the Crown," continued long after that monarch's death, and until the country was deluged with the Wars of Independence. King David's barons and their successors emulated their sovereign's example in founding churches and monasteries throughout the land. Thus we find that at the close of the 12th century one Duncan, Earl of Carrick, to whom the whole country of Carrick had been apportioned by William the Lion, granted some of his lands there to the Abbey of Paisley, under certain conditions: namely, that the monks of Paisley should found a monastery in Carrick after their own Order of Cluny, and that these possessions should at once be handed over to the new community.

On the same terms Earl Duncan granted to Paisley the patronage of the churches of Straiton, Dailly, and St. Oswald of Turnberry and entrusted to its care the books, vestments, and other articles necessary for the use and adornment of the future monastery.

Crossraguel Abbey

The monks of Paisley evaded the conditions of this munificent grant. The Church of Turnberry was confirmed to them by Florence, the Bishop-elect of Glasgow, in 1202; twenty-three years later, Honorius III confirmed to their use the lands of Crossraguel and Southblane; and in 1236 they received a confirmatory grant of the churches of Turnberry, Straiton, and Dalmakeran, from Alexander the Second:

> "Abstract.
>
> Charter by Alexander the second, King of Scots, whereby he grants and confirms the gift which Duncan, the son of Gilbert, Earl of Carrick, made to God and St. James and St. Mirin of Paisley, and the monks there serving God, and to serve for ever, of the churches of Turnberry, Straiton, and Dalmakeran, with all their right pertinents; and also of the five pennyland of Crosragmol and of Sutblan, by their right marches; to be held by the said monks in free, pure, and perpetual alms, as freely as the charter of the said Duncan bears ; reserving the king's service.
>
> Witnesses: Alexander bishop of Moray, Philip of Mubray, Eoger Avenel, David the Marischal, William of Lyndesay, William of Mar', Adam of Logan.
>
> At Edinburgh, 25th August in the 22nd year of King's Reign, 1236."

Meanwhile they built at Crossraguel a cell or oratory, where they had service performed by some of their own community for many years, enjoying all the while the wealthy emoluments of the Carrick lands.

During the visit of Robert II to Carrick in 1374 Abbot Nicolas prevailed upon the king to ratify, at the parish church of Kirkoswald, the three Crown Charters of Robert I. In the lawless districts of Carrick these charters of confirmation must have been literally worth their weight in gold to the monks.

Abbot Nicolas witnessed several charters of the period, notably a most interesting deed by John Kennedy of Dunure to the Chapel of St. Mary of Maybole (remarkable for the fines to be levied upon the presbyters for non-attendance at mass) and another charter, by Roland Kennedy of Blairquhan in 1390.

Nicolas possibly lived to see the great Crossraguel Charter of 1404, signed by Robert III. This was the climax of all preceding grants, the Charter in *liberam regalitatem seu regaliam*, the confirmation of all the Abbey lands and other property to be for ever in a free regality. Among them we find the churches of Kirkoswald, Straiton, Dailly, Girvan, and Kirkcudbright or Ballantrae; the chapels of Kirkdamdie and Chapel Donnan; the various lands granted by previous benefactors, and the island of Ailsa Craig.

Charter by King Robert III, granting to the Monastery of Crossraguel certain Churches and Lands:

"Abstract.

Charter by King Robert the Third, on the ground of charity and for the safety of the souls of all his ancestors and successors, and specially of his own soul and that of his beloved consort Anabella, Queen of Scotland, and of his son David, sometime Duke of Rothesay, Earl of Carrick, and of all the faithful dead, granting and confirming to the abbot and convent of Crossraguel, and the monks there serving God, in perpetuity, all their lands following, that is to say, of the churches of St. Oswald of Turnberry, St. Cuthbert of Straton, St. Cuthbert of Innergarvane, St. Cuthbert of Innertig, and St. Michael of Dalmulkerane: Also the two penny land of the chapel of the Holy Trinity of Kildomine, two mercates of land doted by John Henry, five penny lands of Crossraguel and Southblane, one penny land Channacheth, one penny land called Balekirstenlorcane, and the whole land of Dumheynen, a penny land of Clachrybeg, of Achenacht, of Dallochorane, and Corrale, respectively, five penny lands of Drumgrelach, five merk land of Snade, and one merk of land in the tenement of Donemurthy: Also twenty shilling lands of Drumcaldilthey and Drumfern, twenty shilling lands of the chapel of St. Donnan of Cragach, ten shilling lands of John Makcubyn in the tenement of Trudonag, twenty shilling lands of Drumrachney and of the overlordship of the same tenement: Also the island of Ilysay, with the pertinents; To be holden, had, and possessed, all and sundry the aforenamed lands, by the said aboot and convent for ever, in free regality, in fee and heritage, and in pure and perpetual alms, with gallows and pit, sok, sak, tholl, theme, infangthief, outfangthief, and with the four points pertaining to the crown: Performing therefor, continually and daily, one mass for the soul of the king, and for the souls of all those before mentioned, to be celebrated in the said monastery by one qualified monk, at a particular alter, with a special collect for the king, together with other offerings of devout prayers."

Sealed with the king's seal, and dated at Linlithgow 24th August 1404.

The Abbot of Crossraguel was created absolute sovereign over his whole territory. The grant of regality gave to him all that the Crown had to give, even to the *quatuor punda coronm*, the jurisdiction in cases of murder, fire-raising, rape, and robbery.

Abbot William must have returned from his pilgrimage in 1532, for we find him attending the Parliament of that year which instituted the College of Justice. In 1534 he leased the parsonage fruits of the church of Straiton to James Kennedy of Blairquhan (the first instance of a lease in these documents) and in 1535 he was again in Parliament.

The annexation of the Abbacy of Crossraguel to the Bishopric of Dunblane was ratified by the Parliament of 1633, and eight years later a special Act was passed in favour of Peter Hewatt, the Commendator. By virtue of this, Mr. Hewatt was, in consideration of his advanced age and his inability to support himself and his family, confirmed in the rent of the

Abbacy during his life; with the additional proviso that his family should enjoy it for nineteen years after his decease. He had meanwhile been a minister in Edinburgh but lost his living there in the religious turmoil at the metropolis during the early part of the 17th century, when he had even suffered imprisonment. He died in 1650. The revenues of Crossraguel were therefore enjoyed by the Bishop of Dunblane for a few years. On the final overthrow of Episcopacy in 1689, all that remained of them, consisting of a small property in land, with the patronage of the five churches of Straiton, Ballantrae, Dailly, Kirkoswald, and Girvan, were annexed to the Crown, together with the buildings and "precincts" of the Abbey.

Since the Act of Parliament (1874) abolishing Church patronage, the sole relic of the great Regality of Crossraguel is the small plot of ground enclosing the ruins of what was one of the simplest, yet one of the most beautiful, specimens of Gothic architecture in Scotland.

The territorial estates of the Abbots of Crossraguel were of the largest extent. The greater part of Carrick, or Ayrshire south of the Doon, owed allegiance to them; and from Elsberry Head to Ballantrae, and inland to the parish church of Straiton and the mountainous district which borders upon Kirkcudbrightshire, were to be found at one time lairds, yeomen, and farmers, subject to the royal power with which the monks were invested. The Regality of Crossraguel extended over eight of the parishes of Carrick – Girvan, Dailly, Straiton, Ballantrae, Kirkoswald, Maybole, Kirkmichael, and Barr, the last being in mediaeval times represented by the Chapel of Kirkdominie or Kirkdamdie.

Over the first five of these churches the monks enjoyed exclusive rights. Their property was divided into two separate portions:

1.   the temporality, or the revenue derived from lands and other secular sources;

2.   the spirituality, consisting of the teinds and other emoluments accruing from the ecclesiastical dues of parish churches

The teinds were again sub-divided into the teind sheaves, or the *decimce garhales*, consisting of the tenth sheaf taken from every harvest field; and the vicarial teinds, or *decimw fosni*, of which hay was the principal feature, and which was gathered with the yearly tithes of stock, lambs, calves, and other produce.

This sub-division of Church property in early times was well exemplified in the case of Crossraguel. Of the five churches belonging to the Abbey, over which they could exercise their right of patronage, the monks appointed a vicar, who enjoyed the lesser teinds, to Girvan, Ballantrae and Straiton; while they appropriated to themselves all the revenues of Dailly and Kirkoswald and appointed a chaplain to serve the cure at those churches.

Bull by Clement IV, confirming to the monks of Paisley sundry lands and churches; among others the whole land of Crossraguel and Southblane in Carrick, with their pertinents, by the gift of Duncan, Earl of Carrick. Dated 1269:

> "(Bagimont's Roll). – Taxatio Beneficiarum Freter Prelacias Scotie in decima parte eorundem. –Anno MCCLXXV, In Decanatu de Carrick. Prepositura de Maybole. - Vic. de Maybole, Vic. de Kirkmichell, Vic. de Stratton, Vic. de Innertig, Vic. de Girven, Vic. de Colmonell. Libellus taxationum seu contributionum spiritualitatis conceparum S.D.N. Regi per prelatos et clericos Regni Scotice."

Mr. Abercrumbie, the Episcopal minister of Maybole at the close of the 17th century, thus alludes to it, "In this country religion has had the influence upon the people to dispose them to the founding and endowing many places for devotion; for though there be but one monasterie in all this country, viz. Crossraguel, within two myles of Mayboll, westward ;which, besyd other revenue, enjoyed the tythes of these five parishes, viz. Kirkoswald, Dailie, Girvan, Ballantrae, and Straton; which enjoyed the jurisdiction of regality within itselfe, to which all its vassals and tenants were answerable; yet were there also several other pious foundations and dotations".

Straiton Church remained the property of Crossraguel until the Reformation. The south transept of the old church still stands and is the pew of the Blairquhan family. It is of 13th/14th century workmanship.

90A. *Letter of Tack by Henry and Mary, King and Queen of Scots, to Gilbert Earl of Cassillis of the Abbacy of Crosraguel for 19 years.* —[*10th February* 1565-6.][2]

Oure Soueranis Lord and Lady ordanis ane Letter to be maid undir the Privie Seil in dew forme makand mentioun that thair Majesties understandis that the Abbay of Corsraguell hes evir bene disponit to freindis of the hous of Cassillis at the sute of the erlis thereof for the tyme and for thair gude

service, quhilk abbay is presentlie vacand[1] in thair hienessis handis Throw deceise of umquhile Quintyne last Abbat thairof, and thair Majesties having the lyke gude opinioun of thair traist cousing Gilbert now Erll of Cassillis Lord Kennedy as thair progenitouris hes evir had of his predecessouris ffor his gude trew and thankfull service Settis and for maill Lattis to the said Erll his airis and assignayis all and haill the said Abbay of Corsraguell with all landis kirkis teyndis milnis multuris woddis fisheingis abbey place housis yardis and pertinentis quhatsumeuir pertenyng thairto For all the space and termis of thre yeris nixt following the day and dait heirof quhilk day and dait salbe thair entre In and to the tak and assedatioun of the said abbay and haill fewis thairof and thaireftir to endure be the said space of thre yeris and eftir the outrynning of the saidis thre yeris utheris thre yeris and sua furth fra thre yeris in thre yeris unto the Ische and full compleit end of nyntene yeris With power to the said Erll his airis and assignais To sett and raise all landis kirkis teyndis and possessionis pertenyng to the said abbay siclike and alsfrelie as the said umquhile Abbat mycht have usit or sett the samyn in his lyvetyme or befor ony dispositioun maid of the samyn or ony part thairof to utheris with all and sindrie utheris commoditeis fredomes etc. frelie quietlie but ony revocatioun And that for the yeirlie payment of the soume of sevin hundredth merkis usuale money of Scotland according as the said Erll is detbund to pay be virtew of the tak and assedatioun quhilk he hes sett to him be the said umquhile Abbat[2] quhilk yeirlie dewtie thair Majesteis for the gude service maid and to be maid to thame be thair said cousing[3] Remittis and dischargeis during all the tyme of this present tak and assedatioun Commanding hir hienes Comptrollar present and to cum and all utheris to desist and ceis fra all craving or uptaking of the said yeirlie dewtie Discharging alswa the Lordis of Counsell and Session of all passing and directing of ony letteris aganis the said Erll his airis and assignais the tenentis occupiaris and possessouris of the landis and possessionis of the said abbay for payment of the rentis and dewiteis therof or ony part of the samyn to ony utheris during the tyme of this present tak and assedatioun Attour thair Majesteis for the causis foir-

[1] But we have seen from No. 82 *supra* that it was granted to Allan Stewart by Queen Mary in the previous July. The Earl seems to have been successful in obtaining the King and Queen's signature to this document, which virtually annuls that grant.

[2] No. 77 *supra*.

[3] This Earl of Cassillis was an ardent supporter of Queen Mary, and was present at the battle of Langside, for which his estates were forfeited (Tytler's *History of Scotland*; *Historical Account of the Kennedies*, p. 37).

saidis promittis to the said Erll That he sall have ane confirmatioun of all
sic few landis as he hes in Carrick and Galloway gratis, without ony com-
positioune, and commandis the Thesaurair and remanent Lordis Composi-
touris to pas the samyn confirmationis in maner forsaid And in caise this
present tak be nocht sufficient securitie upoun the said benefice Thair
Majesteis sall reforme the samyn of new gif need be And that the said
Letter be extendit in the best forme with all clausis neidfull Subscrivit be
thair Majesteis At Edinburgh the tent day of Februare the yeir of God
Iⁱᵐ Vᵉ thre scoir fyve yeris.

The above letter of "Tack" (lease) is a rarity in that Gilbert has managed to procure the royal signatures on a document
that overrules a previous lease that he had been forced into. These are the signatures of Queen Mary and King Henry
(Mary, Queen of Scots and Henry, formerly Lord Henry Darnley).

CHURCH OF SCOTLAND – HISTORY

Beginnings

Christianity reached the British Isles through Roman colonisation in the 1st and 2nd centuries AD and continued within
the tribal and cultural mix after the Roman withdrawal in 410 AD. There is archaeological evidence of a Christian
presence at Whithorn associated with Ninian, a shadowy 5th century figure about whom little is known. More
information exists about Columba who, fleeing Ireland, made landfall on Iona in 563 AD. There, with his attendant
monks, he established a community and, using the network of sea and sea-lochs, evangelised as far as Inverness. He also
created a *scriptorium* where sacred texts were copied. Another famous name associated with these early beginnings is
Kentigern, also known as Mungo, patron saint of Glasgow, whose original church is thought to have stood on the site of
today's Glasgow Cathedral. He and Columba were contemporaries.

Columba died in 597 AD. That same year Augustine arrived in Canterbury, sent by Pope Gregory to evangelise, but also
to organise. By the mid-6th century there were two Church traditions within the British Isles – Ionian and Roman. The
former reflected the Celtic pattern associated with Columba, the latter conformed to the customs of Rome. Two specific
points of disagreement involved how the date of Easter was calculated and the style of tonsure, that is, the manner in
which monks shaved their heads. To resolve things a synod was held at Whitby in 664 AD where the Roman practice
prevailed, though another 50 years would pass before Iona complied.

The Middle Ages

The early Church was based around five major episcopal sees – Rome, Constantinople, Antioch, Jerusalem and
Alexandria, but in 1054 a major split occurred. Known as the Great Schism, this saw the Church divide in an east-west
split. Based on its association with the apostle Peter, the Roman Church asserted a primacy which the eastern churches
would not accept; thus, today we have Catholic and Orthodox, Pope and Patriarch. Scotland lay within the western
Catholic Church and famous names from this period include the saintly Queen Margaret, wife of Malcolm III and
mother of three Scottish kings – Edgar, Alexander I and David I.

Iona Abbey

This was the period which saw the building of St. Giles' in Edinburgh, St. Andrews Cathedral, and the great abbeys of Iona, Paisley, Arbroath, the Borders and elsewhere. In 1378 the Catholic Church found itself divided with rival popes in Rome and Avignon. England remained loyal to Rome, but the Scots recognised the Avignon pope, Benedict XIII who in 1413 granted the papal bull which established Scotland's first university at St. Andrews. Four years later the papal schism was healed and in 1472 Pope Sixtus IV raised the See of St. Andrews to an archdiocese. Twenty years later Pope Innocent VIII accorded the same honour to the See of Glasgow.

Reformation

The mediaeval Church had great power, but it also had its critics. One of the issues with which the first Archbishop of Glasgow had to deal was an Ayrshire movement which was challenging Church teaching. Known as 'the Lollards of Kyle' they not only rejected traditional practices; they positively affirmed counter-arguments in favour of priests being allowed to marry (as distinct from turning a blind eye to concubinage) and the right of people to read the Bible and to worship in their own language. 'Lollardy' was a pejorative term (meaning 'muttering'). In Scotland it produced martyrs such as James Resby, burned at the stake in Perth in 1407, and Paul Crawer, who suffered the same fate in St. Andrews in 1433.

In 1517 things came to a head when, according to tradition, Martin Luther nailed his *Ninety-Five Theses* to the door of All Saints Church in his native Wittenberg. Luther's focus was the selling of indulgences which purported to reduce time spent in purgatory, with the proceeds funding the re-building of St. Peter's in Rome. Thanks to the recently invented printing press Luther's ideas quickly spread far and wide. In Scotland they were embraced by people such as Patrick Hamilton who had studied in Germany and was martyred at St. Andrews in 1528. Others took up the cause including George Wishart and his sword-bearer, John Knox. Wishart, too, suffered martyrdom but Knox, strongly influenced by John Calvin from time spent in Geneva, survived to achieve his goal when in August 1560 the Scottish Parliament rejected the authority of the Pope and outlawed Mass. The following year things were complicated (to say the least) by the return from France of Mary, Queen of Scots to assume her throne and adhere personally to the Catholicism in which she had been raised. The aim of Knox and his followers was reform, not the creation of a new Church. Indeed, there were those within the leadership of the pre-Reformation Church, who continued to serve, advocating change from within and giving leadership to the post-Reformation Church.

Priests became ministers, bishops served as superintendents (ministers with a regional remit) and new structures were put in place, though it was not until 1592 that a full Presbyterian system was adopted by the Scottish Church and Parliament.

This comprised an ascending series of courts made up of ministers and elders, namely, Kirk Session, Presbytery, Synod and General Assembly.

Following the murder of her husband, Lord Darnley, and her marriage three months later to the Earl of Bothwell (suspected of involvement in the murder plot), Mary had come under pressure to abdicate in favour of her infant son, James. Her supporters rallied to her cause but, following defeat at the Battle of Langside in 1568, she fled to England where she was imprisoned by Elizabeth and finally executed in 1587. In 1603, on Elizabeth's death, the Crowns of Scotland and England were united under James. His aim was Church uniformity, on Episcopalian lines, north and south of the border. Consequently, during his reign and that of his successors Charles I and II, the Scottish Church alternated between Presbyterianism and Episcopacy. The Stewart kings were strong believers in their divine right to rule both Church and State but they had to reckon with the Covenanters who, in 1638, signed the staunchly Presbyterian National Covenant. Not until 1690, following the 'Glorious Revolution' was the reformed Scottish Church finally settled as Presbyterian, though more trouble lay ahead.

Secession, Disruption and Eventual Re-union

In 1707 the Parliaments of Scotland and England united and it was not long before policies emerged with unsettling consequences for the 1690 settlement. In 1711 legislation was enacted restoring the right of patronage which had been abolished in 1690. This returned power to landowners and town councils to nominate ministers to vacant parishes, thereby removing the right of call from congregations. This was to become the source of much division in the Church over the next century and a half. In 1733, protesting at what they saw as the Church's acquiescence in patronage, several ministers seceded and in 1761 this was followed by a second secession.

Above: The Fathers of The Reformation – Calvin, Farel, Beze and Knox (and an interloper from the Kirk).

In 1843 a far greater schism occurred. Known as the Disruption this resulted in approximately one third of ministers and congregations leaving the Church of Scotland and constituting themselves the Free Church of Scotland. The continuing denial of the right of call to congregations, along with the striking down by the civil courts of Church legislation as *ultra vires*, lay behind this dramatic turn of events.

In 1847 the United Presbyterian Church was constituted by descendants of the previous century's Seceders. Some hard-liners remained apart but, essentially, by the middle of the century Scotland had three significant Presbyterian denominations. In 1874 Parliament finally abolished patronage and this opened the prospect of reunion, though that would take time and, again, be achieved in stages. In 1900 the Free Church and the United Presbyterian Churches came together to constitute the United Free Church which united with the Church of Scotland in 1929.

The 1929 Settlement

The re-uniting of the Church of Scotland was based on two vital principles – the Church's role as a national Church and its spiritual independence in matters relating to doctrine, worship, government, and discipline. Both principles are reflected in a series of Articles Declaratory which set out the Church's constitution and form a schedule to the Church of Scotland Act approved by the Westminster Parliament in 1921. With regard to the national Church role it should be noted that the Church understands this in terms of service rather than status. The Articles refer to a distinctive call and duty to bring the ordinances of religion to the people of every parish of Scotland through a territorial ministry.

The term 'established' is not used, as it is in connection with the Church of England. Nevertheless, the Church retains some historic traditions. The Sovereign is represented each year at the General Assembly by a Lord High Commissioner, who sits in a throne gallery overlooking the Assembly, but does not enter the Assembly itself. While the Sovereign has no role in the government of the Church the Queen has personally attended General Assemblies in 1960, 1969 and 2002 and when in residence at Balmoral Castle, she traditionally worships at Crathie Kirk.

The Articles Declaratory also assert the Church's Catholicity and its Ecumenical commitment. While standing within the Reformed tradition the Church of Scotland also maintains its place within the One Holy, Catholic and Apostolic Church. On this basis, and mindful of Christ's prayer that all his followers should be one, the Church seeks to share with other denominations in Christian mission and service to the people of Scotland.

Recent General Assemblies have also encouraged interfaith dialogue and the Church is a member of Interfaith Scotland as well as of the ecumenical agencies, Action of Churches Together in Scotland (ACTS) and Churches Together in Britain and Ireland (CTBI). The Articles Declaratory also emphasise the global task of 'labouring for the advancement of the Kingdom of God throughout the world' and the Church continues to set a high value on its relationships with partner churches in many countries.

Ordination of Women

In 1966 the General Assembly recognised the eligibility of women for eldership and in 1968 the ministry was opened to women. In 2004 Dr. Alison Elliot became the first woman installed as Moderator of the General Assembly and the first elder to serve as Moderator since the 16th century. In 2016 women represented a little over half of the eldership and approximately one-third of ministers.

St. Cuthbert's of Straiton; The Disruption 1843 and Reunification 1929; Change of Name to Straiton St. Cuthbert's Church

The Disruption of 1843 had no effect on Straiton Church directly; Robert Paton was the Minister at that time, and he remained in his charge. The only effect came from the Reunification in that the Kirk Session was called to a special meeting on 10th March 1929 to vote on a motion on "The basis of incorporating Union between the Church of Scotland and the United Free Church of Scotland". Mr. MacMorland and Mr. Mitchell, elders moved that such an incorporation be approved, and the motion was carried without dissent.

Following confirmation of that approval being passed to Church of Scotland Central Offices, another meeting was called to discuss a change of name so that there would be no confusion with any other church in the new Union which was also dedicated to St. Cuthbert. The meeting of the Kirk Session was held in Straiton Church on 28th July 1929 with a Sederunt of: Rev. J. F. McCallum, Moderator and Messrs. Mitchell, Watson, Calderwood, Crombie and MacMorland (Session Clerk), Elders.

"It was resolved by a majority of votes that the name of the Church be 'The Church of St. Cuthbert, Straiton'".

UNION OF THE PARLIAMENTS 1707

The reasons for the Union of the Parliaments (which was vastly unpopular with the ordinary Scottish people even though most of them at that time did not have the vote) were complex and varied. They can be summarised as follows:

- From the Union of the Crowns in 1603, England and Scotland had one monarch but two Parliaments. While this worked most of the time, there were occasions when the two institutions parted company – such as when England executed King Charles I (to the distress of many in Scotland) and became a republic, while at the same time Scotland's governing body resolved to appoint King Charles II as their monarch. From the perspective of the leaders in London, such a situation had to be avoided in the future and the removal of the Scottish Parliament was seen as a way of achieving this.

- Following the abdication of King James VII and the accession of William and Mary, the Scottish Parliament agreed and declared a few months later that James VII had forfeited the Scottish throne. But there were many in Scotland who still supported the deposed monarch. There were even uprisings in Scotland in support of James and the Jacobite cause was still bubbling away at the turn of the century.

- There was still a large measure of religious intolerance in both England and Scotland and those in power were determined that there should never again be a Catholic monarch, but the deposed Stuart line (with their Catholic sympathies) really had a stronger claim on the throne and again there were more in Scotland who felt that this should count. When the English Parliament decided, without consultation with their Scottish counterparts, that the crown should go via the Electress of Hanover, the German granddaughter of King James VI and through her to her son (the future King George I), the Scots Parliament made plain their resentment.

- There were a number of poor harvests in Scotland in the 1690s and Scotland's economic position was then drastically worsened by the ill-fated Darien Scheme to create a Scottish colony in Panama. Scotland lost 25% of its liquid assets. The Act of Union undertook to pay 400,000 pounds in compensation to those who had incurred these losses. This was of course blatant bribery as the people who were to benefit from this compensation were among those who voted in favour of the Union.

- Scotland relied on 50% of its exports going to England. In an act of blackmail in 1705, the English Parliament closed their market to Scottish cattle, coal and linen and declared that all Scots would be treated as aliens. It showed the vulnerability of Scotland to a trade war. In addition, Scotland was excluded from England's colonial territories – indeed early moves towards the Union of the Parliaments stumbled in England as they were reluctant to allow open access. But the Act of Union in 1707 created the greatest free trade area in the world at that time.

Treaty of the Act of Union 1707

A commission representing the two bodies met and thrashed out the details. The Scots lost the argument for a federal arrangement, but did manage to secure the continuation of the Scottish legal system, education and church. These were important elements in allowing the country to continue to regard itself as a separate entity. The privileges of the Scottish royal burghs were also to be maintained.

Debates in the Scottish Parliament were heated and lengthy while the crowds in the streets burnt copies of the treaty and threw stones at the Parliament windows. A mob held the city of Glasgow for a month. But, on January 16th 1707, the Treaty of Union was passed by 110 votes to 67 (with more than a suspicion that some of the poorer Members of Parliament had been bribed – though this was nothing new for those days). The Treaty was passed in Westminster without opposition and the Scottish Parliament met for the last time on 25th March 1707. When the Act of Union was given the Royal Assent by the Earl of Seafield, he touched the document with the Royal Sceptre saying "There's the end of an auld sang." Nearly 300 years later, at the "re-convening" of Parliament in Edinburgh in 1999, the Presiding Officer was to remark that it was the "start of a new sang".

In his novel *Heart of Midlothian* Sir Walter Scott summed up the attitude of the Scottish "man in the street" at the time in the words of one of his characters, Mrs. Howden: "I dinna ken muckle aboot the Law" – "I ken, when we had a king, and a chancellor, and parliament - men o' our ain, we could aye peeble them wi' stones when they werena gude bairns – But naebody's nails can reach the length o' Lunnon".

THE STORY OF STRAITON KIRK

Originally Told by

Edited and Updated by

The Rev. J. F. McCallum, M.A.
Minister of the Parish
1928–1971

James A. S. Kirk
Elder 1988
(Session Clerk 2003–2015)

Preface to the Original Story by The Rev. J. F. McCallum, M.A.

The writer offers this story of the Kirk at the request of many members and friends of the congregation but claims for it little that is original. Throughout the years, he has learned much from the many visitors, drawn from all walks of life, whom he has conducted over the church. In particular, he owes a debt of gratitude to two friends who gave him invaluable help – the late Rev. Dr. David Easson, a fellow student at St. Andrews, and the late Rev. Dr. William McMillan.

Dr. Easson was a recognised authority on the Medieval Church, and lecturer in Church History in the University of Leeds. Dr. McMillan, Minister of St. Leonard's, Dunfermline, was also an historian of some note. He occupied the pulpit of Straiton in August 1934 and left some notes on the chantry chapel.

Many of the wonderful furnishings and gifts were made or framed by Mr. Hugh Lennox, Prestwick, a member of the congregation, and for many years' estate joiner at Blairquhan.

If, as a result of this short work, the parishioners and members of the congregation come to have a greater appreciation of and deeper reverence for their bonnie Wee Kirk, the writer will feel rewarded.

John F. McCallum,*
Straiton, February 1975.

---

*John Foster McCallum was born on 23rd December 1894, at St. Boswells in the historic County of Roxburgh in the Scottish Borders. John was educated at Morrison's Academy, Crieff and St. Andrews University where he graduated Master of Arts in 1918. He was licensed by the Presbytery of Auchterarder in 1921 and first ordained at Dunnichen, Forfar on 30th October 1923 and transferred to Straiton Parish in Ayrshire on 15th August 1928 where he remained until his retirement in 1971.

Extract from Minutes of Straiton Kirk Session meeting held on the 21st February 1984, Eulogy delivered by Reverend Walter D.M. Moffat, Moderator of the Straiton Kirk Session:

"The Kirk Session record with regret the death on 16th January of the Reverend John F. McCallum, Minister of this Parish from 1928 to 1971.

During his ministry Mr. McCallum showed great interest in the well being off all in the parish, took an active part in the life of the community and cared for the Church with deep devotion.

During his retirement he willingly gave of his services to the Church and Parish, making a worthwhile contribution to many facets of local affairs. Suitable Tribute was paid in Church and at Ayr Presbytery, where he was Clerk from 1946 to 1968.

The Kirk Session give thanks for his gifts he was able to use in his ministry and add that he was not slothful in business but was fervent in spirit serving The Lord."

"Open to me the gates of righteousness:
I will go into them,
and I will praise the Lord."

(King James Version: Psalms – Ch118 V19)

The Parish Church of Straiton is dedicated to Saint Cuthbert (635–687)

Although English Church tradition has in the past promoted the legend that Cuthbert was the son of an Irish king, it is most likely that he was born near Melrose, of poor parents, as it is known that he tended sheep on the hills above the Abbey as a boy.

In the year 651AD, while watching his sheep, he saw the soul of St. Aidan carried to Heaven by angels in a vision. Inspired by this vision he became a monk at the monastery in Melrose and was eventually appointed as its third Prior. From Melrose, he followed the monastery's founder, St. Aidan to Lindisfarne and became the Prior of Lindisfarne, then Bishop of Hexham before returning as Bishop to Lindisfarne.

St. Cuthbert died on 20th March 687 and was buried in his monastery at Lindisfarne. After several moves over the intervening years in 1104 the shrine was transferred to the cathedral at Durham.

There are several churches in Scotland dedicated to St. Cuthbert. The earliest of these is claimed to be Edinburgh St. Cuthbert's at the foot of Lothian Road. The tale is that St. Cuthbert in his travels stopped at the Nor Loch just below Edinburgh Castle and built a small hut in that location, believed to be occupied by the present-day church. A charter granted by King David in 1127 is provided as evidence of the church's existence then or even earlier.

Straiton St. Cuthbert's ancient existence is also verified by a Royal Charter from Alexander II in 1236.

The Church of Saint Cuthbert, Straiton

Straiton Church was founded early in the 13th century by Duncan, Earl of Carrick who granted its patronage to the monks of Paisley Abbey on condition that they erected a monastery of the Cluniac Order in Carrick, to which the church would then be transferred. This was confirmed by King Alexander II in 1236.

Crossraguel Abbey was founded in 1244, and soon afterwards the patronage of Straiton passed to it, as agreed. This was confirmed by Robert de Bruce, grandfather of King Robert the Bruce. The sole interest that either Paisley or Crossraguel monks had in the patronage of Straiton, or any other foundation, was financial. They collected the teinds and any other emoluments of a parish, and in return a vicar paid out of the "lesser teinds", served the parish and, where appropriate, at the chantry altar, though this duty was often assigned to a special priest, with no other commitments. Such was the practice in Straiton. Following the Reformation in 1560, patronage passed to the Crown until 1874 when it was abolished by Act of Parliament.

The present church consists of the main body of the kirk or nave, a distinctive bell tower with vestry accommodation and a chantry chapel, believed to have formed part of the south transept of the original church, which had been partially destroyed by zealots in the early years of the Reformation. The nave was restored in 1758 and again in 1901, when the bell tower and vestry were added.

A further major restoration project of the church buildings has recently been undertaken by the congregation, with the assistance of the Heritage Fund, Historic Environment Scotland, The National Churches Trust, Ayr Presbytery and the Church of Scotland General Trustees. These extensive works commenced in 2018 with roofing, guttering and harling replacement. The work continued in 2019 with new heating and lighting installations and full internal redecoration, including plastering of the old chapel walls.

The Chantry Chapel

The south transept was converted to a chantry chapel by John Kennedy of Blairquhan about 1475. He died in 1501 and a priest from Crossraguel Abbey recited or sang Mass for the repose of John Kennedy's soul. Chantry chapels were founded by lairds in their parish churches or in private chapels of their own. Death and recurring wars, with the devastation that accompanied them, made life insecure, and Dunbar wrote the typical verses of that time, with the refrain, "Timor mortis conturbat me", "The fear of death disturbs me". It was believed that if a priest could say Mass daily for a departed soul then its time in purgatory would be shortened.

Entry to the chapel is by the "Priest's Door" on the west wall. There is an ogee arch above the door and a niche above it where, perhaps, the image of the patron saint once stood. On entering, the stoup for the holy water is on the left; on the east wall is a piscina, for draining the sacred vessels after use; a little further to the right is a credence table on which the vessels were placed before consecration.

Between these two "alcoves" stood the high altar for the dead; a little further to the right, and about two-thirds up the wall is a pedestal on which, presumably, stood an image of the Virgin.

Turning to the south wall, on the left is the ambry, or cupboard, where the sacred vessels and the reserved host were kept. Until a few years ago, this cupboard, or sacrament house as it really is, was sealed up, and when opened it was found to contain a paraffin bottle and a broken lamp funnel, a clear indication that the user, unaware of its real purpose, found the "cupboard" a convenient store house!

Top left: Priest's Door.
Top right: Stoup.
Middle right: Piscina.
Bottom left: Credence table.
Bottom right: Tomb.

The tomb, for which the chantry chapel exists, still bears traces of blue and red, the original and traditional colourings of the period. The recumbent figures, according to the Lyon King, were probably part of a free-standing tomb of a later date and may have been placed on the tomb for safety. The crest is that of the Kennedys of Blairquhan.

The chapel was lit by a fine Gothic window immediately above the tomb. No seating was provided; worshippers either stood or carried their own stool. Along the full length of the west wall is a sedile or stone seat which was reserved for the elderly and infirm, hence the phrase, "the weakest shall go to the wall".

After the Reformation, the chapel was sealed off from the church, and retained as a burial place for the lairds of Blairquhan. This continued to be used until 29th July 1870 when the private cemetery was opened and consecrated in the grounds of Blairquhan. Thus the chapel was not destroyed in the early post-Reformation days.

The Restoration of 1758

The nave or main building of the church was restored and rebuilt. The chapel was re-opened, a roof was thrown over the lower part and the laird's loft, or gallery was built. An outside stone stair led into the retiring room, separated from the gallery, and here the laird and his family had a collation, a "bite of lunch", between services. The gallery had a plastered roof and was lit by two windows broken out on the east wall, while the opening into the church was rectangular, not an archway.

The Restoration of 1901

Chantry Chapel

The gallery, retiring room and stone stair were removed; the windows in the east wall and the external door in the west wall were built up. The priest's door was brought back into use and all the walls were plastered. Pews were set up on two low platforms which covered the old Kennedy family graves, and the centre passage between the two sets of pews was laid with slates taken from an old billiard table at Blairquhan, while the single step from the passage into the main building was laid with stones from an old box mangle at Milton.

A barrel roof replaced the former plastered one, and the chapel was separated from the church by a Gothic arch, built on two old existing pillars, broken in places, perhaps by the supports of the former gallery, and filled in with cement. The Gothic window, hidden from view of worshippers for some 200 years by the former partition, was transformed. A stained-glass window, in memory of Sir Edward Hunter Blair, 4th Baronet of Blairquhan, and his wife Elizabeth Wauchope, was given by their children.

The artist was C. E. Kempe, whose nom-de-plume, a wheat sheaf with two stars, appears in the bottom right hand corner. The subject of the window is Christ Enthroned in Glory with the Latin and Greek forms of the sacred monogram to the left and right. The Four Evangelists, with their appropriate symbols, the angel, the lion, the ox and the eagle, occupy the base.

In the Church of Scotland, the font is usually found on the chancel or near the communion table. Following our baptism, we become members of the Church. Accordingly, the placing of the font at the most ancient door, as here, is correct, symbolising our entry into the Church. The octagonal stone font, with copper basin, was the gift of Sir James Fergusson, Baronet of Kilkerran, Postmaster General at that time, and living at Balbeg. The font is covered with an oak lid, bearing the Fergusson crest, and is a symbol of the time when the water, used in baptism, was believed to have miraculous healing power, hence the tendency to steal it. To guard against this, lids and sometimes padlocks were often used. The following symbols, in relief, are round the font: the Burning Bush; St. Andrew; the Paschal Lamb; the Star of David; (this Jewish symbol may have been included because Jesus "was of the house and lineage of David"); the dove; the fleur de lys; the sacred monogram and the Cross.

A new priest's door of teak replaced the iron gate that had barred the way to the lower part of the chapel when used as a burial place. On removal, it became the garden gate for the former manse.

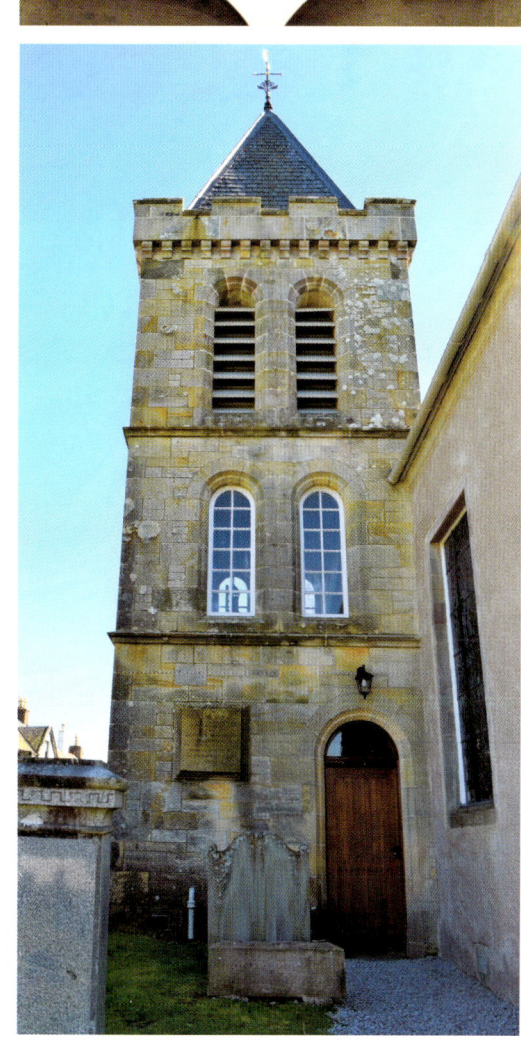

TO THE MEMORY
OF
CAPTAIN DAVID McADAM
49TH REGIMENT
WHO DIED AT TEMPLEMORE
24.. FEBRUARY 1849,
AGED 30 YEARS.
HE SERVED WITH HIS REGIMENT IN CHINA, AND
WAS PRESENT IN THE ACTIONS OF CHUSAN,
WOOSUNG, AND CHING-KIANG-FOO.

THIS TABLET
IS ERECTED BY HIS BROTHER OFFICERS
A MARK OF THEIR GREAT ESTEEM FOR HIM AS A FRII
AND SINCERE REGRET FOR HIS LOSS.

Nave

Prior to 1758 it is not known what the building was like. However, following the rebuild, it was a plain rectangular building with a plastered roof and remained so until the restoration of 1901.

The pulpit and the precentor's box were in the centre of the north wall. There was also an east and west gallery. The only form of heating provided was from a central stove in the passageway in front of the laird's gallery, the iron pipe from the stove projecting through the roof. On either side of the pulpit hung two alms boards listing dates and the names of pious donors, with their gifts of money. It was a common practice of the time to stimulate Christian giving by honouring those who gave such sums to the Church to help the poor of the parish.

On the north wall a tablet had been erected by his fellow officers, as a mark of esteem, to the memory of Captain David McAdam, who died at Templemore, County Tipperary, Ireland, on 14th February 1849. Originally from "Stratton" he is buried in an altar tomb at St. Mary's Church Graveyard in Templemore

The main church building (nave), relatively unchanged from the 1758 rebuild, was completely upgraded during the 1901 restoration. The cost of the restoration was partly met by the heritors, partly by the proceeds from a two days' bazaar in Ayr and by the gift of a parishioner.

Design and plans for this major restoration project, which included the addition of a porch (vestry), belfry within a pseudo-Norman tower, were led and drawn up by John Kinross (1855–1931) an eminent Edinburgh architect and former President of the Edinburgh Architectural Association and a local architect John Murdoch (1825–1907) from Ayr. John Macvicar Anderson, a Glasgow-born London-based architect and the father-in-law of the newly-inducted minister, the Reverend Wellwood Maxwell Landale, acted in a consultative capacity. Scott Morton Architectural & Co were responsible for the craftmanship for the tower, belfry and vestry. The chief contractor on site was Quentin Clark, a master builder and joiner in Ayr.

The old plastered ceiling was replaced by a beautiful collar beam roof of yellow pine. It had been intended that it would have matched that of St. Columba's, London, but it is understood that there were insufficient funds. Beautiful carvings run the whole length of the roof.

To give extra height to the ceiling the floor was lowered three feet, hence the dressed stone parapets round the outside of the church.

A new marble chancel was built and furnished with a beautifully carved oak pulpit, carved oak elders' stalls formed into the woodwork surrounding the chancel and a carved oak communion table with three chairs. The marble of the chancel was a gift from the then minister, the Rev. William Maxwell Lansdale.

The beautifully carved oak pulpit, of Dutch design, was the gift of Mr. Alan. Fergusson, Kilkerran, in memory of his sister.

The punctured eyes of the cherub below the lectern cast a shadow, giving a life-like effect.

The carved grapes are an example of the early Christian church taking over Jewish symbols. Grapes suggest fertility, hence the fruitful preaching of the Word from the pulpit.

It is not known who gave the communion table, the moderator's chair or the elders' stalls, but these so nearly match the pulpit that they may have been one munificent gift. The brass candlesticks were the gift of the Women's Guild.

The pews in both the nave and the chantry chapel are made with red pine. Lighting was from four paraffin lamps, hung from oxidised copper crowns, and was the gift of the minister's sister. In 1939 when electric light was introduced the lamps were removed, but the four crowns were retained. From each of them three period lanterns were dropped, and the crown raised nearer the roof to give a greater spread of light. The old alms boards, stored in the tower since 1901, were cleaned, re-varnished and re-hung in the chapel, with the surplus chains from the lamps. New central heating was introduced from a coal-fired boiler with radiators and pipes.

Entrance to the church is by two studded teak doors at the east and west end of the main building.

Further Repairs to Chapel and Tower, 1964

In this year the plaster on the walls of the chapel was crumbling and discoloured by damp.

The plaster was removed from the chapel walls. It had been hoped that the stonework could have been treated and left free of plaster. Unfortunately, the breaking out of the windows on the east walls, and of the doorway on the west wall in 1758 had damaged the walls, so they had to be re-plastered.

The parapet round the top of the tower was found to be leaking badly. An additional sum of approximately £1,000 was raised and the work was successfully undertaken.

The condition of the plaster on the priest's door was very bad and it was resolved that it should not be renewed, but to effect German pointing, which has given the pleasing effect of dressed stone.

The old pillars, forming the base of the Gothic archway between the chapel and the main building, were painted a stone colour to hide the cement blemishes of 1901. To try and effect a cure for the dampness round the tomb, the soil on the outside of the south wall was excavated, new drainage introduced and the whole filled in with red blaze.

The work of renovation in the tower proved difficult. The whole of the woodwork round the parapet had perished. To renew it, the slates on the spire had to be stripped off before the work could be undertaken.

Slates were replaced and a new heavy drop pipe from the parapet was passed down through the tower to a new drain.

Mr. Harry Taylor, A.R.I.B.A., Architect to the Church of Scotland Home Board and cousin of well-known local Nurse Taylor (Margaret), advised as to the renovation work, and particularly the special treatment of the priest's door. An electric boiler was installed to replace the old coal-fired boiler, with original radiators and pipes being retained. The two studded teak doors at the west and east gables of the nave remained as the main access for worshippers. The chantry chapel is entered by the priest's door on the west wall of the chapel.

The vestry and belfry are accessed by a door at the base of the tower, and access to the belfry is via a steep winding staircase. The pulpit is entered from here via a small set of steps and there is a door for entry to the nave.

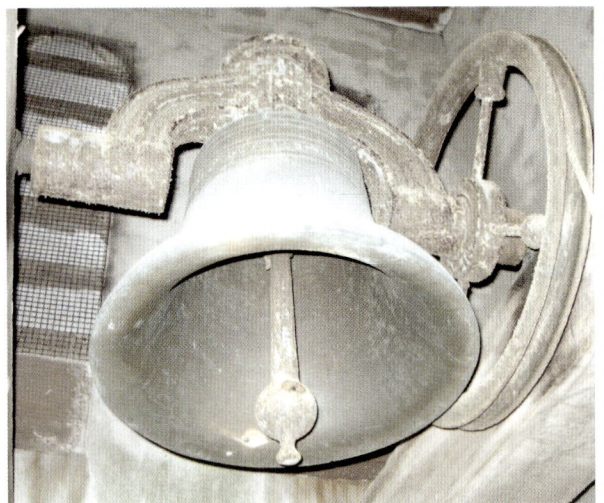

There is also a bell in the belfry above the west door. It continued to be rung for many years after the new bell was installed, until this small external belfry required attention, after which the new bell was regularly rung.

Until 1971 three bells were rung each Sunday morning: the first at 9 am to waken the parishioners, the second at 11 am, the Readers' Bell, the third at 12 noon, indicating the canonical hour of worship.

In early post-Reformation days priests were in short supply; their place was taken by readers who might be the village schoolmasters, until the itinerant priest arrived. Hence the laird's collation between services.

The main bell in the tower belfry is now rung only once each Sunday, by the duty elder, to call worshippers to our regular 12 noon service of Word and Sacrament.

The tower, in the style of pseudo-Norman architecture, and bell were gifted by Quentin McAdam, of Dalmorton, in memory of his parents.

On the north wall of the tower there is a granite slab (below) on which are inscribed the names of volunteers of the parish who fought in the First World War (1914–1918). The Latin text translates as "Let Him Who Has Won the Palm Carry It." This was Lord Nelson's motto.

Top left: Priest's Door.

Top right: Studded teak door, east gable.

Middle left: Studded teak door, west gable.

Middle right: Door to vestry.

Bottom right: Old belfry, west gable.

Bicentenary of the Main Building

In September 1958, a special service of Thanksgiving marked this bicentenary. It was conducted by the Moderator of Presbytery the Rev. James MacMorland, M.A., B.D., a native of the parish and son of the late William MacMorland who was schoolmaster and session clerk for over 50 years, and the minister, the Rev. J. F. McCallum, M.A., who also took part in the Quincentenary Service some 17 years later, having retired in 1971. During the service the following gifts were dedicated:

The Main Building: A manual-operated blower for the pipe organ was purchased in 1915, the gift of James and Jean McKie and relatives, an old Straiton family. The pipe organ was replaced in 1983 with an electric organ, which itself was replaced with a more modern version in 1994; **Three patens for use at Communion**, the gift of Mr. R.W. and Mrs. Craig, Riverside, in memory of their grandson, James Berry Craig, drowned in Loch Lomond; **a framed scroll of the Ministers of the Parish since the Reformation** the gift of Mr. Hugh and Mrs. Lennox, Prestwick, members of the congregation; **electric lighting for the West Gallery**, the gift of the Straiton branch of the S.W.R.I.; **psalter and hymn book, for use at the organ**, the gift of an elder; **hymn books for Sunday School use**, the gift of Mr. A. S. and Mrs. MacMeikan, Police Station, Straiton; and **a set of white book markers**, the gift of Mrs. James White, Milton.

Quincentenary of The Chantry Chapel

On Sunday 22nd June 1975 a service was held to mark the conversion and adoption of the chantry chapel 500 years previously by John Kennedy of Blairquhan.

The service was held in the evening at 6pm and was conducted by clergy (past and present) from Paisley Abbey, Ayr Presbytery and Straiton St. Cuthbert's by the Rev. W.D.M. Moffat. Mr. James Hunter Blair of Blairquan also took part. The brochure indicates that praise was led by Mr. George McPhee, organist from Paisley Abbey along with the choristers from the Abbey. However, the remaining copy of the order of service has the praise being led by Mr. Martin Doole, assistant organist at Paisley Abbey.

Commemoration Service

Sunday, 22nd June, 1975 at 6 p.m.

Conducted by

The Rev. JAMES D. ROSS, M.A.,
Minister at Paisley Abbey

The Rev. IAN M. TWEEDLIE, B.Sc., B.D.,
Moderator of Presbytery

The Rev. J. F. McCALLUM, M.A.,
Minister at Straiton, 1928-1971

The Rev. W. D. M. MOFFAT, M.A.,
Present Minister

Mr. JAMES HUNTER BLAIR, D.L.,
Blairquhan

•

Mr. GEORGE McPHEE, B.Mus., F.R.C.O.
Organist and Master of the Choristers
with Choristers from Paisley Abbey

ST. CUTHBERT'S PARISH CHURCH
STRAITON

QUINCENTENARY

OF CHAPEL

1475 - 1975

Other Additional Gifts and Furnishings Since 1901

Over the years members and friends of the congregation have, by their gifts, sought to enrich the beauty of the church. The following is a list of such furnishings and gifts:-

The Chapel: Three chairs for the baptistry (1965) bearing three symbols from the font – the Sacred Monogram, the dove and the Burning Bush, the gift of the Rev. J. F. McCallum in memory of his sister, Kate.

Wrought-iron Pedestal and Vase for Flowers (1973), the gift of the elders' wives.

Memorial Mural Tablets:

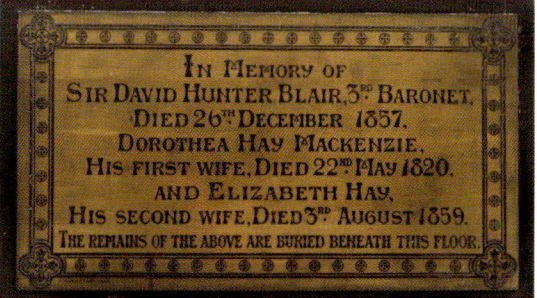

West Wall

East Wall One

East Wall Two

West Wall: In memory of Sir David Hunter Blair, 3rd Baronet, died 26th December 1857; his first wife, Dorothea Hay Mackenzie, died 22nd May 1820; and Elizabeth Hay, his second wife, died 3rd August 1859.

East Wall One: In loving memory of John Hunter Blair, died 25th January 1937, aged 71, eighth son of the late Sir Edward Hunter Blair, 4th Baronet of Blairquhan.

East Wall Two: In loving memory of Gaspar Patrick Hunter Blair, Commander, Royal Navy, younger son of Sir Edward Hunter Blair, Baronet of Blairquhan, killed in action off the Isle of Crete, June 1st 1941, age 45 years.

The Main Building:

The table lectern and Bible (1923), the gift of Mrs. Landale in memory of her sister, Mary Anderson. The donor had suggested brass offertory plates in place of the old ladles, which were worn and in need of repair, but the Kirk Session wished the use of the ladles to be continued and had them repaired.

Oak ladles inlaid with ebony (1939). By this time the two ladles, made of Memel fir, were very badly worn, and Mr. and Mrs. McWhirter, Linfairn, presented two new ones. These hang beside the pulpit and are still in regular use. The older ones now hang in the chapel and were last used at the bicentenary service in 1958. The use of ladles dates to pre-Reformation times.

After 1901 admission to the east gallery was by the east outside door only. Consequently, the people's offerings could not be uplifted by ladle from this gallery. A small velvet bag was used for which Mr. William Mitchell, Bennan, an elder, was responsible. After his death in 1936 the uplifting of the offerings presented difficulties, and sometimes no offerings were received.

Opening of service door to East Gallery (1936). Owing to the floor of the main building having been lowered three feet a stone wall behind the panelling made opening operations difficult and demanded very skilled work, but the door was fitted, and steps dropped to floor level in the church. So that the door might be secure when in use, the tongue of the lock was checked to engage in an ingeniously fashioned 'keep' on the wall.

So once more the ladle appeared in the east gallery.

> "And when they made him elder,
> Wi' the ladle it was grand
> To see him work the wester laft
> And never miss a man!"

The Landale Window (1939), the gift of Mrs. Landale, in memory of her husband, minister of the parish (1899–1928). The subject is the Good Shepherd, including scenes from the Life of Christ, and at the base St. Martin sharing his cloak with the beggar. The artist was the late Herbert Hendrie A.R.C.A. of Edinburgh College of Art, whose other works can be seen in Liverpool Cathedral. The window was dedicated on 29th March 1939. Mrs. Lansdale unveiled the beautiful stained-glass window and Reverend David Swan B.D., Minister at Maybole preached the sermon with a reading from 2nd Timothy Chapter 2 verse 15.

Pencil drawing of the church, hanging near the Landale Window, is the work, drawn in 1889, of the late Mr. Tom Cassels, an Ayr architect with a Straiton connection. It shows the iron pipe from the heating stove projecting through the roof, and the outside stairway leading to the laird's gallery and retiring room. Note the crow-stepped gable of the chapel's south wall. No cross appears above the Gothic window. Could it have been destroyed in the post-Reformation violence? The drawing was presented by Mr. David B. Cassels, Ayr.

Thursday
8 april   Blairquhan

Dear mr kirk,

I was so very pleased
to get yesterday from
Gerald Jones a perfectly
splendid picture of Straiton
kirk in 1889, showing
the stairs up to what
was, then the "Lairds Loft"
for Blairquhan and those
who lived there and the

staff. My father remembered
these arrangements well, and
the sheepdogs which, then,
accompanied their owners to
the Service.

It is beautifully framed.
and will be kept on show
here permanently as a
reminder of things past.

I would like to
thank you very very much.

your sincerely
James Hunter Blair

In 2004 a framed copy of this pencil drawing was presented to Mr. James Hunter Blair for hanging in Blairquhan. As noted in his letter of appreciation (copied above) he was delighted to receive this print and confirmed his memory of his father being in the laird's loft with the other heritors and their sheepdogs at church services.

Fabric donation box (1939) placed near the chancel. It is beautifully executed in oak and superimposed on an oak shield, matching those on the pulpit, all made from a piece of oak, salvaged when about to be broken up for firewood!

Two memorial chairs (1946) in oak for use at the Communion Table. One bears the St. Andrew's Cross and a thistle, the other the St. George's Cross and a rose. They were given by the Rev. J. F. McCallum and his sisters in memory of their parents.

The Pulpit Bible, given to the Rev. Robert Walker on his admission to the parish in 1738. When he was called to Edinburgh in 1746 he took the Bible with him. No more was heard of it until 1817. In that year Dr. Paul became minister and it was returned to him by a friend. For many years the Bible was kept in the manse attic until returned to the church in 1948. The Bible was used for the Scripture readings at the bicentenary service in 1958.

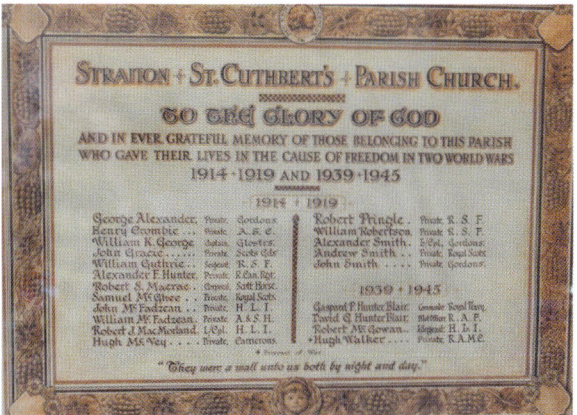

War Memorial (1948) framed in oak. The names of the Fallen in two world wars are inscribed on vellum, bordered with the pulpit carving and the church's emblem. The artist, David Palmer, of Edinburgh, was concerned as to who was to frame his work. When told that the village joiner, Hugh Lennox, had been commissioned, he said, "Pray, be careful", but when shown the photographs of some of the joiner's work, replied, "I think he'll do". The text is from I Samuel XXV.16 "They were a wall unto us both by night and by day." Mrs. Lambert, of Longcroft, a war widow, unveiled the memorial.

British Legion Colours (1949). In that year an approach was made to the Kirkmichael and Straiton joint branch of the British Legion for permission to hang their Colours in the church. The request was readily granted, on condition that the Colours would be equally shared with Kirkmichael Church, the 'change over day' to be Remembrance Sunday in each year. The Colours were hung in Straiton for the first time on Sunday 27th March 1949.

Communion Plate: Two silver communion cups, believed to be the gift of the Crown, inscribed "For the Kirk of Stratin". These cups date to the early part of the 17th century and are still in use today. They are stored in a secure location, between Communion services. The Sacrament of Holy Communion is held twice a year on the first Sunday of June and November.

In 1954 a legacy bequeathed to the church by Miss Isabella Kilgour, of Ayr, and formerly of Straiton, enabled the Kirk Session to fulfil her wish to provide individual Communion cups. Three patens are used for the elements, donated by Mr. and Mrs. Craig.

Two small pewter plates, part of his maternal grandfather's dinner set, were given by Mr. McCallum, to be used as patens. The remaining Communion plate is of ordinary type, in common use in Scotland in the 18th century.

A white linen cloth, which covers the table at the celebration of Communion, was the gift of the late Mrs. Dunlop, Knockbride.

Two recumbent crosses holding several metal tokens, dated 1823, were given by Miss Kathleen M. Blair, a relative of the Rev. John Blair, minister of the parish (1844–1898).

Water installed (1952). The Victory Fund Committee provided a gravitation supply of water to the tower, where, until then, water had been carried in pails up the narrow and awkward stair to a hand-fed cistern. Because of the difficulties, the water level in the cistern was often at a dangerously low level for the heating system.

Two praise boards (1958) were the gift of Mr. Leslie Norman, Craigfad, in memory of his wife, Ada Margaret.

Framed oak Lennox Scroll (1959) acknowledges the skilled craftsmanship and great service rendered to the church by Mr. Hugh Lennox. If ever there was a case of the hour producing the man, this is surely it. The Scroll is the work of the Ayr County Council's Architect Department. Mr. Lennox has continued to serve the church with his great skill and devoted service since 1959.

Pulpit pendant light (1959), the gift of Miss Espie, formerly of Straiton, and Cumnor Hall, Ayr, in memory of her parents.

Two offertory plates (1963) were gifted by the late Mr. A. C. White and Mrs. White, Traboyack, for use at special services.

The following is a list of Easter gifts, presented by the Bible Class over the years:

1937 – Two brass flower vases for the Communion Table. The vases were believed to have been stolen from the church in 1994, but thanks to the eagle eye of Mrs. Jean Dickson they were recovered some months later and collected from Cumnock Police.

1938 – Pulpit Bible, psalter and hymn book. The Pulpit Bible was inscribed by the late Mr. Duncan MacCallum, Campbeltown, cousin of the minister's father, and father of Mrs. Hugh Lennox. This was replaced with a new Bible in 1987, gifted by the family in memory of Winnie Allan. In 2003 a grateful Kirk Session accepted an offer from the Grant family to provide copies of the *New Revised English Bible* to be placed in every pew for use of the congregation as well as providing a new *Revised Version Pulpit Bible*, suitably inscribed in memory of Jimmy Grant, a "True Country Character".

1939 – Striplight for the organ.

1940 – Electric fire for the vestry.

1963 – Oak table for visitors' hymn books.

Royal Letter of Presentation (1963) of the Rev. John Blair. He was the last presentee of the Crown, the Act of 1874 having abolished patronage. Noteworthy are the replica of the Privy Seal, and the guinea stamp, recalling the lines of Burns:

> "The rank is but guinea's stamp
> The man's the gowd for a' that."

The letter, along with Mr. Blair's pulpit gown in perfect condition, was presented by Miss Kathleen M Blair, of Seahouses, Northumberland, and Mr. Randal B Cooke, grandson of the Rev. John Blair.

The letter and seal were framed by Mr. Donald Ashcroft, Craigengower, and hung by him, assisted by Mr. Robert P. Rae, The Cottage, Straiton.

Runner for Communion Table (1966). This lovely cover was donated by David and Mary Kidd on behalf of their granddaughter Dr. Samantha Clark and inscribed "From Sam in memory of her Mum Gillian, Easter 2003". This cover remains on the Communion Table for most of our regular services, throughout the year. The cover that it replaced was the gift of Mr. and Mrs. Jackson, from York, who were at that time living in Straiton, in commemoration of the baptism of their son, Alistair, in Straiton St. Cuthbert's Church. Mrs. Jackson made the runner, but the embroidery is the work of the Guild of Seamstresses at York Minster, colour Presbyterian blue; this cover is still used, mainly at special services over Christmas, New Year and weddings where larger floral displays are placed on the table.

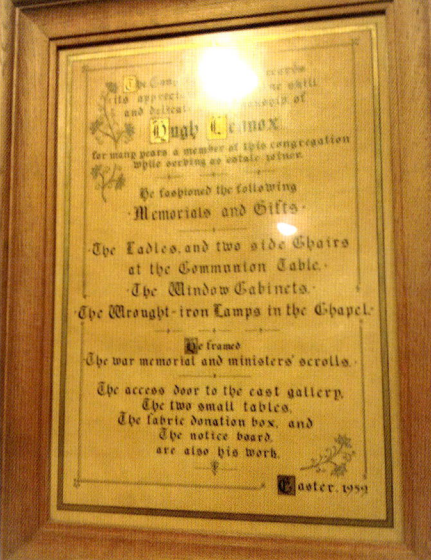

Top left: Pulpit light.
Top right: Framed Lennox Scroll.
Middle left: Royal Letter of Presentation.
Middle right: Brass flower vase.
Bottom left: Table lectern.
Bottom right: Runner on Communion Table.

The McWhirter Window (1977), the gift of the late Mrs. Davidson, Ayr, formerly Daisy McWhirter of Linfairn and Genoch, "In Memory of her many friends". Its theme The Light of the World, showing God's creative hands over His Son's head; the Son, with right hand raised in blessing standing upon the earth with its seas, stars and moon; behind Him the flaming sun, source of light and life; the Church in the midst, spreading God's Word; growing corn and vines, elements of Communion, renewing man's faith and granting him new grace.

The new window was designed by Scottish artist Sadie McLellan signed and dated 1977 and was unveiled and dedicated by the Rev. W.D.M. Moffat on Sunday 9th October that year. The Kirk Session agreed to pay for a memorial plaque, suitably inscribed and placed below the window.

Both the church's stained-glass windows were examined during the preparation of the various condition reports prior to commencing the process for the planned restoration work (which finally got under way in 2016 in terms of funding applications and permissions etc.). It was decided, due to the noticeable deterioration in the Landale Window supports and noticeable bowing of the panes, to call in some expert assistance. With the support of Patrick Lorimer, of ARPL Architects, Rainbow Glass Studios of Prestwick were invited to inspect and provide quotations.

It was confirmed that the five saddle bars were all showing signs of significant rust and with the severe corrosion exhibiting in one of the two vertical bars and that within a very short space of time they would not be able to support the window. We were advised that the Landale Window would have to be removed and repaired at Rainbow's workshop. Fortunately, the McWhirter Window was in good shape and only required cleaning up and refixing of part of the glass design which had dropped off and could therefore be worked on *in situ*.

The work was approved by the Kirk Session. The Landale Window was removed very carefully pane by pane by Rainbow on 4th June 2014 and replaced on 29th July 2014, all under the supervision of Patrick Lorimer. The Kirk Session confirmed their satisfaction on completion and thanked Rainbow Glass for their expert and sensitive handling of the restoration of our lovely Lansdale Window. The McWhirter Window was subsequently cleaned and repaired in January 2015.

Two brass flower vases (1999), gift of Mr. and Mrs. David Kidd, Maybole in memory of their daughter Gillian Clark (1959–1998) of Craigbrae, Straiton. The vases were dedicated for use in the church on Sunday 25th November 1999 by Rev. W.G. Jones.

Portable ramp (2000). A mobile ramp was purchased to improve wheelchair and funeral access at the main entry to the church, via the door on the west gable. The step was repaired, and fixings made, by Hubert Thomson of Kirkmichael who gave of his time and materials as a gift to the church.

Pew cushion fund (gift from the congregation and community – 2006). It had been agreed at a Kirk Session meeting on 19th March 2006 that cushions for the pews be considered to improve overall comfort of the congregation and it was agreed that a general appeal should be launched, with a starting figure from the Fabric Fund.

Pew cushions (2006–2007). The pew cushion appeal was so well supported by everyone that our target was reached within a year and in 2007 the pews were all fitted with made to measure cushions thanks to the generosity of so many members of the congregation, local community and friends of Straiton.

Church notice board (2006). A new church notice board was gifted by the family of William "Bill" Munro (husband of Mrs. Jean Munro an elder in our church) and suitably inscribed to his memory, dedicated 16th April 2006.

CH4 hymn books (2007). The Church of Scotland was moving to the new Faith edition of the *Church Hymnary* (CH4) and the Kirk Session gratefully accepted the gift of 80 normal and 20 large print versions for use in the church, from the Shearlaw family of High Garphar, Straiton, in memory of the late Robert Shearlaw.

Lectern stand (2008), the gift of Mrs. Harriet Henry in memory of her beloved Jack Henry an elder of our church who passed away on 18th September 2006. Dedicated at the Easter Service on Sunday 23d March 2008 by Rev. W.G. Jones.

- IN MEMORIAM -

BOBBIE SHEARLAW

1920 - 2007

BUCCLEUCH ESTATES
DRUMLANRIG

HIGH GARPHAR
STRAITON

'WE STAND ON THE
SHOULDERS OF THOSE
WHO HAVE GONE BEFORE US'

Top left: Pew cushions.

Top right: Brass flower vases.

Bottom left: Pew bible inscription.

Bottom right: Lectern stand.

Mobile bookcase and display cabinet (2010). These beautiful items of church furniture were gifted to the church by the family of Mrs. Jean Munro, an elder of this church who passed away in January 2010. The display cabinet holds the old Pulpit Bible first used in the church in 1738. At this time additional CH4 hymn books were purchased from the remaining balance of the "Jack Henry Fund".

Praise boards (2010). Two new praise boards were donated by the family in memory of their mother Mrs. Betty Grant. These were securely put in place by Peter Holden, a local joiner.

Tower. In the vestry there are two photographs hanging: the Rev. John Blair Minister at Straiton from 1844 until his death in 1898, the gift of the late Mrs. Dunlop, Knockbride and the Kirk Session, (March 1971). The latter taken outside at the Gothic window in a lovely ideal setting by Mr. Fred. G. Sykes, a Royal photographer, at that time living in Straiton. It was inscribed by James Murdoch, Knockdon, age 12 years; and framed by Alex McFadzean, son of David McFadzean, elder.

Humbly we give thanks to God that for over 700 years men and women have gathered for worship in this sacred place; and that for the most of those years part, at least, of the present church building has stood sentinel, guarding against the enemies of the Faith during religious storms that raged over the centuries, particularly during the "killing times" when the Covenanters stood firm for the faith of their fathers, like Thomas McHaffie, who, while fleeing from the hunting dragoons of the "bloody Bruce", was shot at Linfairn. Now his ashes rest in peace in the quiet of the churchyard.

In these days of social and industrial unrest the visitor who turns aside from the busy world will find himself in tune with the Infinite and the spirits of an age long past, as he enters the peace of this little shrine to "worship the Lord in the beauty of holiness."

"For by grace are ye saved through faith, and that not of yourselves; it is the gift of God".
New English Bible: – Ephesians 2:8

IN MEMORY OF
JEAN MUNRO
1938 - 2010
AN ELDER AND TREASURER
IN THIS CONGREGATION

THE REV. JOHN BLAIR,
PARISH CHURCH STRATON.

HYMNS
127
268
540
603
456

Top left: Mobile bookcase.

Top right: Rev. John Blair.

Middle lef: Display cabinet.

Bottom left: Memorial plaque.

Bottom right: Praise board.

Two hallmarked silver Communion cups (17th Century)

These Communion cups, believed to be the gift of the Crown and still in use today, are inscribed on the base: 'FOR THE KIRK OF STRATIN'.

It is not known which Stewart King presented these cups dated by their hallmarks to 1621. King James V1 reigned until 1625 and was succeeded by his son Charles 1 in that year and held the throne until his execution on 30th January 1649. It is known that Charles made his first visit to Scotland in 1633.

According to the hallmarks the cups were made by silversmith Gilbert Kirkwoode and assayed in Edinburgh in 1621. The third mark is the punch of James Dennieston, who was Deacon of the Guild 1619–1621.

The three marks on the cups represent from left to right: the maker's mark – the Assay Office mark – the Deacon of the Guild mark.

Note: The indents on the top of the cup indicate where the samples have been taken by the Assay Office.

Maker: Gilbert Kirkwoode: Edinburgh, 1609–1645, son of Patrick Kirkwood, blacksmith in Colinton, and Elspeth Foulis. Booked apprentice to his mother's relative, George Foulis, 19th September 1598. Freeman 13th September 1609. His second wife, whom he married c.1618, was his kinswoman, Margaret, daughter of his former master. Deacon and deacon-convener 1623–1625. Bought Pilrig estate 1634 and built Pilrig House by 1638. Died 1645 during an outbreak of plague in the city. He was the master, but not the father, of Thomas Kirkwood, goldsmith.

Goldsmiths have worked in Edinburgh since at least the 12th century. By the late 15th century there were enough of them to have formed their own incorporation, or trade body. The incorporation controlled all aspects of its members' work, including admission to the craft, but most importantly the assaying and marking of their work. These marks – called hallmarks, as they were actually struck in the goldsmith's own hall, guaranteed that their customers were buying wares made of gold or silver of the agreed legal standard of fineness. The Incorporation of Goldsmiths of the City of Edinburgh is therefore the oldest surviving consumer protection organisation in the country!

Since 1457, the Deacon, or leader of the craft, assayed and marked the members' wares, but in 1681 a separate Assay Master was appointed to oversee this task. The Incorporation's importance in the life of the city and country was confirmed in 1687 when King James VII granted it a Royal Charter. In 1784 Edinburgh's Assay Office was made officially responsible for assaying and marking the work of goldsmiths and silversmiths throughout Scotland. Between 1819 and 1964 a second assay office operated in Glasgow, but since that date, the Incorporation of Goldsmiths of Edinburgh has continued to operate Scotland's only Assay Office.

The Chapel. Two wrought-iron standard lamps, the gifts of the Rev. J. F. McCallum and his sister in memory of their sister, Jeanie Stewart.

Vicars and Ministers of
Straiton Parish Church

Before the Reformation in 1560 vicars were appointed to Straiton Church by the Abbot of Crossraguel who held patronage, the right of a patron to appoint the minister in each parish, among other rights relating to the income.

The first recorded vicar or minister of "St. Cuthbert of Straiton" (without any additional access or research into the Roman Catholic Church archives pre-Reformation) is Andrew McCormyll, confirmed in the Charters of Crossraguel as "Vicar of Straiton", who in his capacity as notary in Ayr, signed a document described as:

> "Notarial Instrument upon the resignation of Duncan Fergusson of Knockgarron by staff and baton in the hands of the Venerable Colin, Abbot of Crossraguel and convent of the Monastery thereof, with due reverence, of his forty shilling lands of Knokgarron and Altycaple, lying in the Earldom of Carrick and shire of Ayr: So that it should be lawful to the said Abbot and convent , after the resignation, to dispose freely of the said lands, and especially in favour of John Fergusson, son and apparent heir of the said Duncan, if they should so please to bestow the lands upon him".

This document was noted "Done in the chapter-house of the said monastery, about noon, on the 27th day of August 1490, before these witnesses: John Fergusson, brother of the said Duncan, Duncan Kirkpatrick, John Fergusson son of the resigner, Sir Thomas McIlhauch of Girvan and John Wishart, son and apparent heir of Adam Wishart, burgess of Ayr.

Andrew McCormyll, Notary.

Sir Andrew McCormyll
(1470) 1490

"Vicar of Straiton" from at least before 1490, possibly 1470 onwards. According to the Obits of around the 15th century for the Church of St. John the Baptist in Ayr it appeared that he had been appointed a notary in Ayr at least before 22nd March 1470. On his appointment as a notary he signed the following statement (translated from Latin):

> "And as I was, however, Andrew McCormyll priest of the Diocese of Glasgow [Straiton Church was lying in the Diocese of Glasgow at that time] and received the Royal Notary is to draw the public by order of the authorities as long as each and every one, because of the land, so that all the rest of the resignation is above said, and was going on, and the place would become one, without any witnesses, I was among this kind of all things in general and particular is thus made, I knew and heard, and took a note in accordance with this public Instrument of my own hand, written, and have made the sign of, and the name of my use and wont to here, me, with the signature signed it at the request of, and sought out, and to the belief of the witnesses on the premises".

Sir Andrew McCormyll's own Obit was also included in the book Obits of St. John the Baptist. He died on 3rd April 1507 and it was noted that he "gave to God, the Psalters and Choristers of Ayr, and poor, twenty shillings of annual revenue from his tenements in Ayr distributed in perpetuity at the discretion of the Principal Priest".

The following persons are denoted as "Vicar of Straiton" in various legal papers of the Kennedy family, Earls of Cassillis covering assedations (leases) and tacks (ground rents or tithes). Information has been ascertained on the authenticity or background of these "Vicars" or "Ministers" as far as possible and dates have been verified only by the knowledge that they were stated to be incumbent at the time of their signing documents.

Thomas Boswell
1520

Possibly succeeded Sir Andrew McCormyll in 1507–1508. No record or verification of any vicar appointed between 1507 and 1520. On 22nd June 1522, signed at Straiton, Thomas Boswell, Vicar of Straiton, gave "discharge to Gilbert Maknoil in name of Gilbert Earl of Cassillis of 5merks of the Candlemas term (stipend) 1520 and £10 of the Beltan term immediately following". It can be assumed that he was in post at least in 1520 or even earlier. He was still vicar on 18th August 1539 when he signed another discharge at Straiton in favour of Andrew McLellan and Gilbert Macneil of the sum of £23 as the mail of the vicarage at Straiton.

William Boswell
1562

No record or verification of any vicar appointed between 1539 and 1561. On 28th November 1562 at Perth William Boswell "Vicar of Straiton" gave "discharge to Mr. Patrick Vaus of Cascreoch, in behalf of Gilbert Earl of Cassillis, the sum of 200 merks being the stipend due by the Earl to him the said William Boswell at Martinmas 1562, and for which sum the said Patrick Vaus and the Abbot of Glenluce were enacted in the books of Council to have paid as follows – viz. 40 merks at Michaelmas, and the remainder at Martinmas then last". William Boswell was recorded as minister at Inverkeithing from 1560–1562, so we can assume that this was his first stipend settlement after transferring.

Henry Macalzean
1566

Again, there is no record of appointment since the departure of William Boswell in 1562 until 1566 when Henry Macalzean arrived. Not a lot is known about this "Vicar of Straiton". However, he did sign a rather complicated contract and legal instrument which appeared to tie him in for at least three years and he did not last a full two. The first document was a contract signed at Maybole on 30th June 1566 viz:

> "Contract between Gilbert Earl of Cassillis and Mr. Henry Macalzean Vicar of Straiton, by which Mr. Henry Macalzean lets to the Earl his heirs male and assignees, the teinds fruits profits duties and emoluments of the Vicarage of Straiton, with the manse glebe houses and church land thereof. As sometime possessed by Mr. William Boswell late Vicar of Straiton – for the space of 3 years from the feast of Beltan then last, and at the ish (expiry) of the said 3 years the said Mr. Henry Macalzean obliges him to let to the Earl and his aforesaid, the said teinds fruits, rents, profits duties and emoluments of the said Vicarage, manse, glebe, houses and church land thereof, for other 3 years, and so on from 3 years to 3 years during the life of the said Mr. Henry Macalzean – the Earl paying yearly therefore to him the sum of £50 money of Scotland at two terms in the year, Midsummer, and St. Andrews day, by equal portions, beginning the first terms payment at Midsummer then last – As also Mr. Henry Macalzean obliges him to dispone In feu farm, to the Earl and his aforesaid, the glebe and Church land of Straiton, for payment yearly of 6 merks, together with 3 shillings 4 pence in augmention, and these two sums to be paid along with the £50 at the terms respectively above mentioned the Earl being always obliged to obtain the consent of the Abbot and Convent of Crossragwell to the Charter to be granted by the said Mr. Henry Macalzean in his Lordships

favor of the said glebe and church land And his Lordship further obliges him to pay instantly (in hand) to Mr. Henry Macalzean the terms mail due at Midsummer then last, being the first payment, together with 100 merks, and also £10 in name of grassum, and over and above to give him a horse worth £20.

30 Jun 1566

Witnesses – Hugh Kennedy of Barquhony and John Kennedy of Monunsioun. Dated at Mayboll.

Instrument of *Seisin propriis manibus in favor of Gilbert Earl of Cassillis, in the glebe and church land of Straiten, being a half merk land and lying in the Earldom of Carrick – given by Mr. Henry Macalzean Vicar of Straiton in implement of the Charter granted by him to his Lordship – Seisin given to his Lordship personally, 30 Jun 1566 in presence of Hugh Kennedy of Barquhony, Gilbert Kennedy son of William Kennedy of Fairniganoch and David Kennedy son of the deceased Charles Kennedy of Auchinflower. Dated at Maybole.

John Knox visited Carrick and tried his best to influence people to make changes to the new Church and doctrine. The Kirks in Carrick were some of the slowest in Lowland Scotland to adopt the ways of the full Presbyterian Church. It would appear that Knox's visit to Carrick was not too successful at that time.

John McQuorne
1568

Believed to be possibly the last appointment to the vicarage under the patronage of Crossraguel Abbey or it may have been Henry Macalzean. However, as can be deduced from his later ministry he certainly embraced the new doctrine of the "True Religion". Formerly exhorter at Straiton before being entered at Beltein (festival) in 1568. In 1574 he had also Maybole, Kirkbryde, and Kirkmichael under his charge; was on a committee nominated by the Privy Council 6th March 1589, for the preservation of true religion in the Sheriffdom of Carrick; still minister in 1597, and died previous to 30th May 1598. [*Reg. Min.*; Calderwood s *Hist.*, IV. 570.]

John McQuorne, M.A. (Glasgow, 1589)
1598

Admitted to Dalmellington in 1591; translated to Maybole in 1595; presented to the vicarage by James VI. 30th May 1598. As noted above his father had been nominated to Straiton by the Privy Council in 1568 and in 1574, to ensure that congregations were being adequately served, groups of parishes were created under the care of a single minister assisted by one or more readers. Thus, John McQuorne Senior was charged with the oversight of the combined parishes of Straiton, Kirkmichael, Maybole and Kirkbride. In this work he was assisted by readers, Mr. Matthew Hamilton at Maybole and Kirkbride, William Hunter at Kirkmichael (from 1576) and John Anderson at Straiton.

His son, Mr. John McQuorne, a graduate of Glasgow University (1589), who began his ministerial career at Dalmellington, was translated to the charge at Maybole and Kirkbride in 1595, while his father continued at Straiton. In 1597, by Act of Parliament, the connections of Kirkbride and Maybole with the nunnery of North Berwick ended with its suppression. On his father's death, Mr. McQuorne was presented to Straiton by King James VI on 30th May 1598.

---

*According to this Instrument (a feudal fiefdom or fee given by his own hand), the glebe and church land of Straiton are to be "holden by the Earl for payment yearly of £4 money of Scotland. As the old feuduty and 3 shillings 4 pence like money in augmentation of the rental – to be paid at the feasts of Pentecost and St. Martin by equal portions."

Even among the clergy themselves not a few were favourable to the Royal side, but the fear of exposure kept all save the more reckless from avowing their sentiments. The libels brought against the ministers of Straiton, Auchinleck, Muirkirk, Monkton, and several others, supply a graphic picture of the period.

The Rev. Mr. John McQuorn, minister of Straiton, then aged and paralytic was enjoined by the Presbytery on 27th June 1642, to get "ane helper in respect of the laichnes and infirmitie of his voyce". Later, on 26th November 1645, according to the Presbytery meeting he was accused of "scandalous carriage, in frequenting the alehouses about the village from morning till night during the week, with the exception of a short period about noon, when he went home and took a sleep; being sometimes so drunk that he could not examine his parishioners, after their coming, according to appointment, long distances for the purpose". But the main gist of the charges was his speaking disrespectfully of the Rebellion.

He had said that it was "unlawful to take up arms against the king (alluding to the invasion of England under General Leslie); for, if we wanted the king, the church would be without a head; that the covenant with England was unlawful; that we had nothing to do but keep our own league; and that he did not understand what the people had taken up arms for, seeing that the king had given them all they wanted."

It was also proven against him that he was in the habit of "nicknaming them (the Covenanters) as Puritans." At examinations he would say, to the individual catechised, "Are ye a Puritan? Will ye say the Lord's Prayer or bid God speid?" If they answered "yes," then he would reply, "ye are no Puritan."

It was farther established against McQuorn as evincing his warm side to the enterprise of Montrose, that when the edict was read in the Kirk, calling on the people to assemble at Maybole, he abode in the pulpit silent, and afterwards adjourned with the "malignants" to the alehouse, where they drank, smoked tobacco, and indulged in "horrible swearing" against the cause of the covenant.

As a result of being found guilty of all charges laid before the court he was deposed on that date 26th November 1645, as recorded in the minute and the original indictment "He usuallie frequents the aill-house, drinking indiffirentlie with all sorts of persons from morning to night, except a little in the midst of the day, when he goes home to take a sleep".

He married Jean McQuhirtour, widow of James Chalmers. She died July 1635 and had issue James; Samuel; Jean; Elizabeth (marriage contract 23rd November 1636, Thomas M Blane in Camragen). [*Reg. Assiy.*; *Ayr Sess. Reg*; *Glasg. Tests*; *Booke of the Kirk*; Calderwood *s Hist.*, vii. 385; *Reg. of Deeds*, dxiv. 318.]

Hew Ecclles, M.A. (Edinburgh 20th, July 1638)
1644

Called unanimously, and admitted (colleague) 28th August 1644; presented to the vicarage by Charles I. March 1647; died March 1662, aged about 44. He married Anna, daughter of William Cockburn, minister of Kirkmichael. She survived him, and had issue William, served heir, 19th February 1663; Anna. [*Reg. Sec. Sig.*; *Baillie s Lett*; *Glasg. Tests*; *Inq. Ret. Gen.*, 4677, Ayr, 622.]

David McQuorne
1662

Admitted to Alloway before 1636; presented by Charles II on 11th September 1662; still minister 7th April 1664. He married Margaret Annand, who survived him, and had issue a daughter (married Adam Blair); a daughter (married John

Rankine of Blook); Sara (married David M Querne, minister of Kirkmabreck). [*Reg. Sec. Sig.; Ayr Sheriff-Court Books*, 20th October 1682.]

George Meik, M.A. (St. Andrews, 23rd July 1672)
1683

Educated at St. Salvator's College; passed trials before the Presbytery there, and had a testimonial for licence 18th August 1675; was an expectant, 31st August 1679; admitted minister of Coylton before 12th December 1682; Translated here in 1683; deserted his charge in 1689. [*Kettins Sess. Reg.; Ayr Sheriff Court Books*, 30th, January 1683.]

Alexander Kennedy
1691

Born 1663, son of John Kennedy of Dalmorton; licensed by Presbytery of Ayr 27th April 1688; called July 1689; ordained on 27th January 1691; he was immediately commissioned to the north, and acted a conspicuous part in supplying the church of Foveran, under the auspices of the Presbytery of Aberdeen, and the protection of Alexander Udny of Udny's servants, and armed dragoons.

As well as being the minister at Straiton he was chaplain to the seventh Earl of Cassillis, at whose funeral he officiated in 1701. During the funeral he is said to have exorcised the devil, who had settled on the coffin in the shape of a black crow!

He died before 16th March 1737. He acquired the estate of Knockgray, Kirkcudbright. He married (1) 13th January 1691, Elizabeth Chalmers of Bonnington, who died 1710, and had, issue John of Knockgray; Adam, licentiate, died in 1738: (2) Jean Crawford, who died 17th September 1763, and had issue Anna. [*Glasg. Tests; Spalding Club Miss*, ii.]

The family of Kennedy of Knockgray, in the Stewartry of Kirkcudbright, is descended from the Rev. Alexander Kennedy. His great-great-granddaughter, Anne, married, 10th September 1781, John-Clark, Esq. of Nunland, also in the Stewartry of Kirkcudbright, and their eldest son, Colonel Alexander Clark Kennedy, succeeded, in 1835, to the estate of Knockgray.

An honourable augmentation was granted to his arms in commemoration of his heroics, when in command of the centre squadron of the Royal Dragoons at the Battle of Waterloo, he captured the eagle and colours of the 105th regiment of French infantry "with his own hand".

Robert Walker
1738

Called unanimously 8th June and ordained on 14th September 1738; translated to Second Charge, South Leith on 20th November 1746. The Bible that was presented to him at his ordination and used in that service was taken with him to his new charge. This old Pulpit Bible was later to be returned to one of his successors, Rev. John Paul.

John McDermeit [Fergusshill] M.A. (Glasgow 1746)
1749

Born 1724, son of John McDermeit, minister of Ayr; licensed by Presbytery of Ayr on 21st December 1748; called 23rd February and ordained on 3rd August 1749; he assumed the name of Fergusshill; died 13th September 1793.

He married 11th January 1762, Agnes (died at Largs, 20th June 1818, aged 81), daughter of William McJerrow of Altanalbany, and had issue John, born 24th April 1763; William, born 12th December 1764; Giles, born 25th December 1766; Janet, born 27th February 1769 (married 27th March 1796, Andrew Wilson, merchant, Renfrew); Agnes, born 29th January 1771 (married William Crawford, D.D., minister of this parish); Jean, born 12th January 1773; Robert, born 17th September 1775; Helen, born 23rd May 1778, died 7th March 1828.

William Crawford D.D. (St. Andrews, 3rd February 1810)
1791

Probably fourth son of William Crawford, farmer, New Cumnock; educated at University of Glasgow; licensed by Presbytery of Hamilton on 24th April 1787; presented by George III 9th November 1790; ordained (assistant and successor) 21st April 1791; resigned 2nd October 1816, on appointment as Professor of Moral Philosophy, St. Andrews; died 23rd September 1822, aged 60.

He married 6th February 1792, Agnes, daughter of John McDermeit, minister of this parish, and had issue William, born 23rd October 1793; Agnes, born 21st March 1795; John McDermeit, born 4th December 1796; Andrew, born 29th May 1798; Elizabeth, born 6th August 1799, died 30th December 1813; Robert, born 13th February 1802; George (twin), born 13th February 1802; Alexander, born 29th October 1804; Thomas Jackson, D.D., Professor of Divinity, Edinburgh, born 13th February 1812. Reverend Crawford was author of the chapter on Straiton for the 1792 *Statistical Account of Scotland* where he was noted as "Assistant to the Reverend John McDermeit".

John Paul
1817

Presented by George, Prince Regent, on 6th November 1816; ordained 1st May 1817; translated to Maybole 4th September 1823.

Robert Paton
1824

Presented by George IV on 15th September 1823; ordained 22nd April 1824; translated to St. David's Parish, Glasgow, 11th April 1844. He was author of the chapter on Straiton Parish included in the 1837 *New Statistical Account of Scotland*.

John Blair B.A. (Glasgow 1839)
1844

Born 30th January 1821, son of Thomas Blair, minister of Colmonell; licensed by Presbytery of Stranraer; presented by Queen Victoria; ordained 25th July 1844; died 21st October 1898. He was the last minister to be presented by the monarch. A copy of The Royal Letter of Presentation is framed and is affixed to the wall of the nave, to the right of the organ. A portrait of him is hung the vestry. He was married at Dalmorton on 7th April 1847, by the Rev. Thomas Blair, to Jean (died 20th February 1916), daughter of Quintin Macadam, Dalmorton, Ayrshire, and had issue Margaret Elizabeth, born 13th March 1848; Thomas, born 14th October 1849; Quintin, born 28th October 1851; Anna McFadzean, born 19th July 1853; John Henry, born 23rd May 1855; Jane Macadam, born 11th June 1857; Catherine Jane, born 25th August 1859; James Andrew, born 24th January 1862; Henrietta Ritchie (twin), born 24th January 1862 (died 9th February 1890).

Wellwood Maxwell Landale M.A. (Edinburgh)1892
1899

Born 24th June 1870, son of David Landale, minister of Applegarth; educated at Fettes College; licensed by Presbytery of Lochmaben 1896; assistant at St. Giles, Edinburgh, 1897; ordained 20th April 1899. Married on 16th July 1902, Agnes Frances, daughter of John Macvicar Anderson, architect, London. He was declared by the Presbytery of Ayr *jure develuto* and translated from Straiton (Q.V.) on 15th February 1928 to Penicuik. His first wife Agnes died 9th June 1928 and he married Jessie, second daughter of Robert Muirhead of Northern Lights Commission at Lasswade 30th April 1931 and demitted his ministry on 30th June 1935. He died suddenly on 19th September 1936 at a football match between Hibernian and Heart of Midlothian, an Edinburgh Derby which was the 9th game of the season for both teams in front of a 27,471 crowd. It is not known whether Rev. Landale had a heart condition that brought his life to an untimely end just five days after his 65th birthday. What we do know is that it was a very exciting match with both teams having scored twice in the first half and ending 2-2 at halftime. Both teams went all out for the winner and Heart of Midlothian scored through Andrew Black in the 80th minute. However, with just one minute left in the match William Black of Hibernian scored to make it 3-3 at full time. We can only surmise that unfortunately, at some point the excitement of the match could have been too much for him.

John Foster McCallum M.A. (St. Andrews) 1918
1928

Born 23rd December 1894, son of Archibald M McCallum and Keturah Taylor; educated at Morrison's Academy, Crieff and St. Andrews University, graduating MA in October 1918. Licensed by the Presbytery of Auchterarder May 1921; assistant at Inveresk; ordained 30th October 1923 translated to Straiton 15th August 1928 and retired 1971. Following his retiral he stayed on at the manse, taking an active part in the local community. He continued to make himself available for visitors to the church on a Sunday afternoon, providing short tours with a detailed explanation of the church and its history. He died on 16th January 1984 in his 89th Year.

Walter Donald McKechnie Moffat M.A. (Glasgow) 1941
1971

Born in Canada in 1918 his family had returned to Scotland while he was still of school age, and he was educated at Carrick Academy in Maybole. He was ordained in 1942 at Darvel Easton Memorial Church and left Darvel in 1948 to become minister at St. Paul's Church in Rosemount, Aberdeen. He moved on to Buckie North Church in 1954, where he was very active in the local community and was also president of Buckie Rotary Club. After almost five years in Buckie he accepted a call to Glasgow and was inducted to Glasgow Bellahouston on 10th June 1959.

Following twelve faithful years of ministering to his flock at Glasgow Bellahouston, Walter was called to the linked charge of Kirkmichael with Straiton (St. Cuthbert's) and was inducted to his new charge on 8th July 1971 as the first minister of the new linkage. Rev. Moffat resided in the Old Manse at Kirkmichael as agreed under the terms of the Linkage Deed between Straiton and Kirkmichael Churches. He was moderator of Ayr Presbytery 1978–1979.

In 1942 he married his first wife, Mary Weir Alan, who died in 1983. On 27th December 1984 he married Agnes Poole Johnstone (Nan) who had served as deputy town clerk in Musselburgh, circa 1971 until the 1975 local government organisation.

Demitted (retiral because of age) on 31st May 1985 and died at Musselburgh on 13th January 1987.

W. Gerald Jones M.A. (Glasgow) 1978, B.D. (Glasgow) 1982, Th.M. (Princetown)1983
1985

"I heard the Lord saying, 'Whom shall I send? Who will go for us?' I said: 'Here am I! Send me.'
ISAIAH Chapter 6 – Verse 8

Inducted to Straiton 23rd October 1985. Moderator of Ayr Presbytery September 1997–1998. On Sunday 24th October 2010 a joint service of the Linked Charge of Kirkmichael with Straiton to mark Gerald's Silver Jubilee was held in Straiton St. Cuthbert's Parish Church, the service being conducted by Rev. Dr. John Lochrie BSc, B.D. Th.M. PhD. The Reverend Gerald Jones was inducted to the Linked Charge of Kirkmichael with Straiton (St. Cuthbert's) on 23rd October 1985. The induction was conducted by the then Moderator of Ayr Presbytery, the Rev. A.M. McPhail, B.A. of Ayr Wallacetown Church assisted by Rev. Gordon Macrae, B.D. of St. Quivox Parish Church and the Presbytery Clerk, the

Rev. C.L. Johnston. The service took place in our beautiful church here in Straiton, at 7.00 pm on Wednesday 23rd October 1985. The next evening a welcoming social was held in the McCosh Hall in Kirkmichael, chaired by the Rev. Ian McDonald of Tarbolton. It was especially pleasing for Gerald that the Reverend McDonald was able to attend the Linked Charge Elders Communion Service conducted by Gerald on the Sunday evening of his Silver Jubilee.

A native of Kilbirnie, Gerald graduated with honours in both Arts and Divinity from the University of Glasgow. He was then appointed Peter Marshall Scholar at Princeton Theological Seminary, New Jersey, USA, where he graduated Master of Theology in 1983.

Returning to Scotland Gerald was appointed Assistant Minister of Glasgow Cathedral where he was ordained in June 1984. Thereafter the call came to him from the charge of Kirkmichael with Straiton (St. Cuthbert's), where his family had long associations with Blairquhan and as we say the rest is history. Gerald was honoured to be appointed Moderator of the Presbytery of Ayr in 1997.

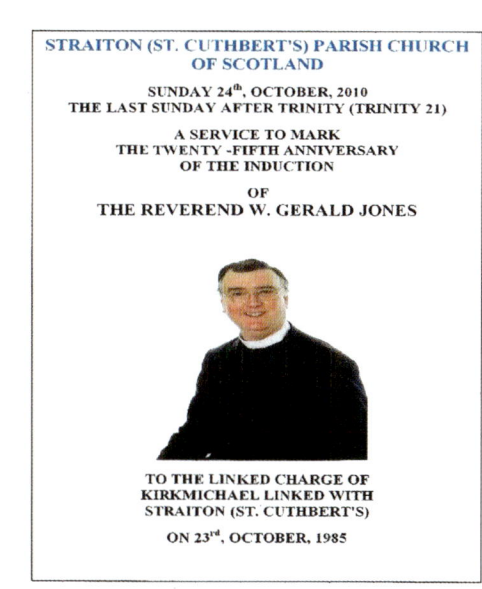

OLD PULPIT BIBLE
Rev. Robert Walker Minister at Straiton 1738–1746

The Pulpit Bible, given to the Rev. Robert Walker on his admission to the parish in 1738. When he was called to Edinburgh in 1749 he took the Bible with him, and no more was heard of it till 1817 when Dr. Paul became minister. An advocate friend of his later that year was browsing among the books on a bookseller's stall in Edinburgh, when he discovered the Bible and returned it to Straiton. Every minister since, on his admission to the parish, has signed it.

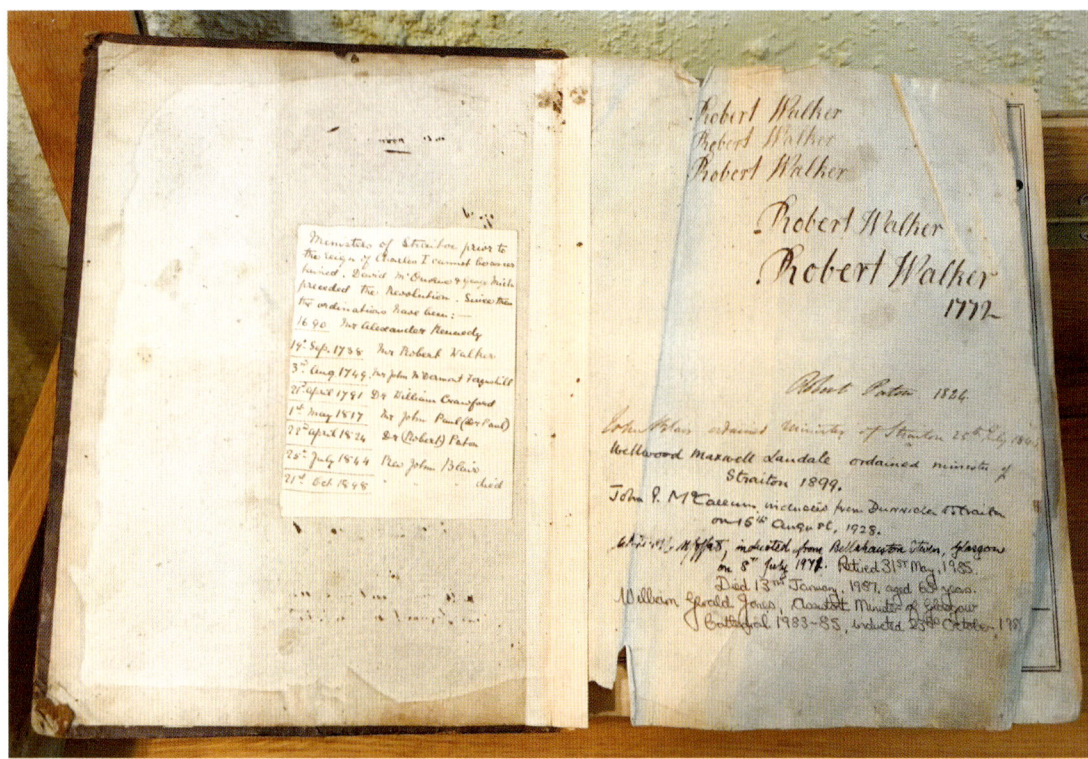

The handmade paper, badly worn in parts through use, has been replaced from other editions, so that the book is kept "somewhat of a curiosity". For many years the Bible was kept in the manse attic, but was returned to the church in 1948, and the lessons were read from it at the bicentenary service in 1958. This Bible is unique in that it is made up of two separate printed editions with (as the cover pages of the Old and New Testaments show) two parts being printed in different years.

Attention was first drawn to this anomaly, when the Bible was placed in the new display cabinet (dedicated to the memory of Jean Munro) and the commemorative plaque (which had been made in 1948 when the Bible was brought back into the church and fixed to a small ledge, made by Hugh Lennox), was fixed to the cabinet. The plaque bore the legend that this Bible was first used in the church on 14th September 1738 (the date of ordination of Rev. Robert Walker). This was confirmed by checking Kirk Session Minutes. Yet the Bible was printed in 1769?

Further examination then showed that the New Testament Section had been printed in London (not Edinburgh as the main part was) in 1702. Mystery solved! It was also discovered that Rev. Walker had written on the back of the New Testament cover page 1702 section and that some other had notated the story of the Bible's disappearance and return. The Rev. Robert Paton has signed at the foot of the page.

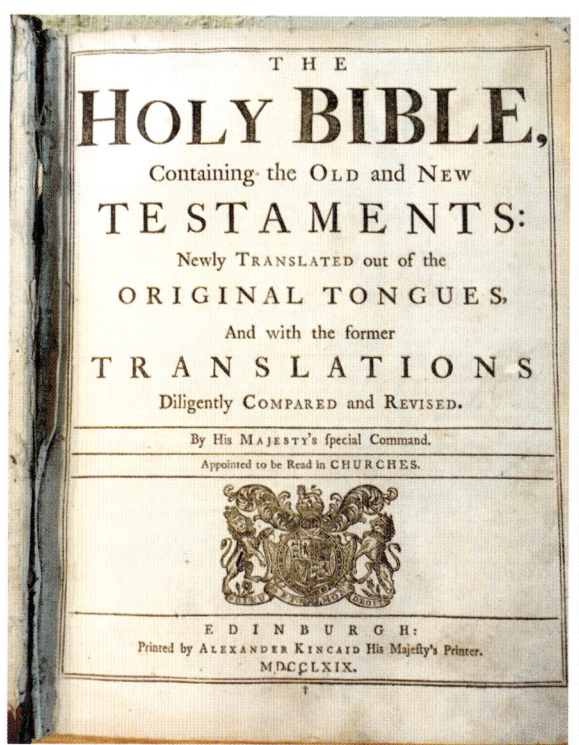

Printed in Edinburgh MDCCLXIX
(1769)

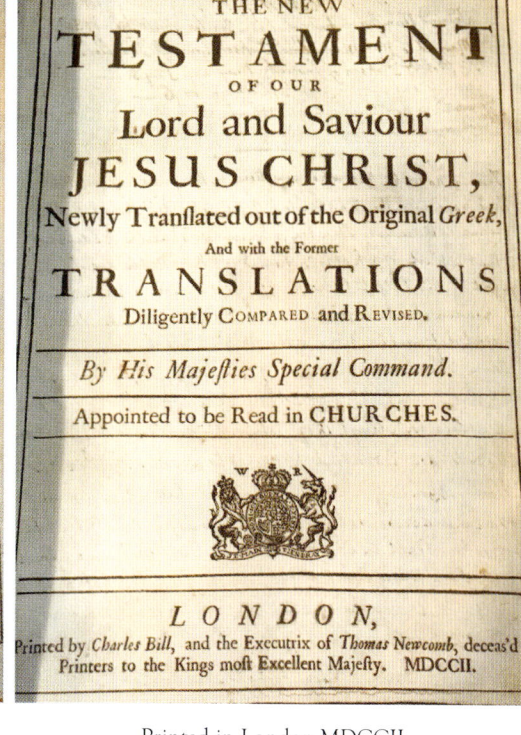

Printed in London MDCCII
(1702)

Notations incorporated in the 1702 Section

Transcript of the Notations: First part: "This Book Belongs to Robert Walker, born February 14th 1716. Ordained Minister of the Gospel at Straiton September 14th 1738, married to Miss Magdalene Dickson younger Daughter to Sir Robert Dickson of Inveresk May 27th 1943 – Admitted to South Leith November 20th 1746 – Transported to the city of Edinburgh and admitted to be Minister of the Congregation belonging to the new Church there October 11th 1754"

Second part: "There is no doubt that what is written in the preceding part of this page is in the handwriting of the late Robert Walker formerly Minister of Straiton, & afterwards of Leith, Edinburgh & that a part of what is contained in this Bible did form part of his Pulpit Bible in his first Parish. Upon examination it however will be found that this Book is made up of several different Editions of the Bible, but by whom is not known. The History of this book so far as can be ascertained is the following.

At the Ordination of the Reverend John Paul at Straiton May 1st 1817 John McFarlane Esquire of Kirkton, Advocate in Edinburgh happened to accompany the Reverend Sir Henry Moncreiff. In the course of the succeeding summer Mr.

McFarlane accidentally picked up a copy of the Bible at a Booksellers stall in Edinburgh, & seeing Mr. Walkers name upon it, knowing him to have been Minister at Straiton he transmitted it to Rev. Paul as the Remembrance of Rev. Walker. Rev. Paul left it to his successor The Reverend Mr. Paton, it is hoped it will be handed down as somewhat of a curiosity to each succeeding Minister of the Parish of Straiton".

Entered at foot of page: "The Reverend Robert Paton, Minister of Straiton 22nd April 1824".

TRABOYACK HOUSE
The former manse at Straiton, Ayrshire

This photograph of Straiton Manse, taken in the third quarter of the 19th century, shows the house shut in closely by trees. The pediment has a circular window and there is still a chimney above it. The ground in front of the house is level, the sharp shelving slope to the lawn being a later alteration.

A more modern photograph of Traboyack House on page 62, which was taken in 2010, shows the full extent of the external changes and improvements made to the property by its first non-Church of Scotland owner, Mr. Anthony White. The chimney on the roof above the pediment has been removed and a new porch constructed (this replaced an earlier late-Victorian style porch which had been added at some point after the old photograph was taken). The house at the time of purchase was not white harled but was of a local sandstone from a depleted quarry at Maybole. Finding stone to match that of the house proved to be difficult. However, eventually some was found in Dumfriesshire. The whole building has now been returned to a whitewash harling finish.

Out of this world and into Straiton or so it seems to the stranger travelling there, a mere 14 miles from Ayr. Yet the bus takes almost an hour to meander along the Carrick byways, so that by the time it reaches its destination the traveller feels that he has been on a great journey. But it's a pleasant journey and its end is equally pleasant – the neat little village of Straiton, its two rows of tidy houses laid out in the mid-18th century by the Earl of Cassillis and looking as if they haven't changed a great deal since then; although in fact they have, for the original houses were single-storey and thatched, while today's houses mostly have upstairs windows and are all slated.

For Mr. and Mrs. Anthony White, Straiton had been 'home' for some nineteen years. Before they made their permanent home there, while they were living in Ayr, they owned a cottage in the village and spent a great deal of time in it. Although so close to the county town, Straiton is in a very different country from its coastal neighbour. While Ayr can be dry and sunny, Straiton, often equally sunny, can also be blanketed in snow; and the day that Ayr receives a smattering of raindrops from a passing cloud can find Straiton wreathed in mist and drizzle, but it's not always an unkindly crime, for the surrounding hills that can attract the rain can also provide shelter.

Straiton has long had connection with the Church. In pre-Reformation days almost the whole of Ayrshire, south of the Doon, was within the regality of the monks at Crossraguel; and parts of the church building in Straiton date back as far as 1350, though it is mainly 18th century with 19th century renovations.

Straiton suffered when the Highland Host marched into Ayrshire at the beginning of 1678 and for fourteen days 800 men were quartered there, "their continual trade" being "shoaling of sheep, robbing men and women night and day, and perfect thieving and stealing."

The earliest mentioned manse was built for the Rev. Dr. John McDermeit, who was ordained at Straiton in 1749. His assistant and successor, Rev. Dr. William Crawford, who was ordained in 1791 and later became Professor of Moral Philosophy at St. Andrews University, wrote the entry for the *Statistical Account of Scotland* 1792, in which he said that the manse "though built so lately as 1753, is in very bad repair".

The writer of the *New Statistical Account* entry in 1837, the Rev. Robert Paton, said that the manse, "which is a plain building, of the size common in 1795, when it was erected, is striking in situation and is a pleasant residence in summer". This still holds true today, though it applies now "all the year round" instead of merely "in summer".

This 1795 manse was built directly in front of, or at right angles to, the earlier one, for some of the back premises of what is today Traboyack House are obviously of great age, so presumably could have been part of Rev. McDermeit's manse, if not of an even earlier building.

Although Straiton Manse had been lived in continuously over the years a minister's stipend could not, perhaps fortunately in some respects, keep pace with the whims of furnishing fashions and house alterations; the house Mr. and Mrs. White bought in 1955 was, apart from some minor renovations, more or less the house that was built in 1795. At the time of the sale, the Church of Scotland was proposing to build a new manse because this old one was in poor condition but, as the Whites said afterwards, had they realised just how poor a condition they might never have bought the place! But buy it they did, and in spite of the heavy cost of restoration they feel that the pleasure of living in the house has justified the effort. One particularly enjoyable aspect of living with the rehabilitation (which is what Mr. and Mrs. White and their two daughters did, camping around from room to room in considerable discomfort) was that when the building was stripped to its bones it was possible to see just how an 18th-century house was constructed.

The old manse fell happily into the right hands, for Mr. and Mrs. White, while keen on the creature comforts provided by central heating and up-to-date plumbing and wiring, were equally enthusiastic about maintaining the 18th-century characteristics of the house, which to them were possibly its greatest attraction. As the place was wringing wet, cold and dark, renovations fell naturally under three essential headings to provide dryness, warmth and light. The first drawback was that no contractor was prepared to estimate for the necessary work, the attitude being that "you just never know what you might run into in a house like this, or how much work might be involved". So Mr. and Mrs. White had simply to trust their tradesmen and it all worked out very well, the work done being of a high standard. Another fortunate factor during that first year was the weather, it was a glorious summer without any real rain for more than six weeks. Although the tradesmen disappeared for the two weeks of the Glasgow Fair holiday in July, by the time the wet season came the roof had been re-lined and re-stated with the old slates. The major problem was damp, so after the roof the next part of the 'drying' process was concentrated on the walls. The sandstone of which the house is built is exceptionally porous, and some earlier attempt at rain proofing had been made by harling the south-west gable. Inside, walls had been too tightly strapped, so penetrating wet had wrought its inevitable effect on the plaster, which was crumbling away. The answer to all this was to strip off the harl, then pick and point the complete stonework and give the south-west gable, which takes the worst of the weather, a silicone spray, which lasts for about seven years, so has been re-done twice already. A vertical damp course was run from foundations to roof for the main outside walls, and for some inside ones too; and some nine-tenths of the plaster had to be renewed.

The manse had always been a cold house a former visitor remembered, being told to put on his coat when going upstairs to look at some papers with the minister! But that has been changed by oil-fired central heating; the unit being installed in a store built to replace back premises that had been pulled down before the Whites bought the house.

Fortunately, most of the woodwork was in a good state – doors, beams and roof timbers are all Memel fir, which woodworm dislike, but about half of the upstairs flooring, plus, attic stairs, was badly wormed, so bad to be replaced, along with the beam above the drawing room ceiling which had bent under the load it had been carrying.

The 'light' giving part of the operation was perhaps the most straightforward, all the old, decayed window frames being replaced by new ones with exactly the same 18th-century style panes and astragals. A French window was made in the little study behind the drawing room, and the rather dark dining room given a completely new side window; while pale and neutral shades have been used in decorating the rooms.

The master bedroom gained an extra view of the hills when a pointed roof was knocked off the minister's study in the single-storey extension at the rear.

Lastly there had to be a new name for the house. Former manses are generally known as Old Manse, with the place-name prefixed; but the Church of Scotland General Trustees made it one of the conditions of sale that the name of the property be changed after purchase from Church ownership.

There was, however, a very suitable old local name, Traboyack, believed to be a corruption of the Gaelic "ri toabh a 'bhoglaich" meaning beside the bog, which does indeed describe the situation of the house. So Traboyack House it has become.

Traboyack House was later lived in for several years by a lady who after her husband died, lived as a recluse and was rarely sighted within the community. Once again Traboyack house fell into disrepair and apart from some replacement of harling in 1982, no major maintenance was done on the property.

Fortunately, it has been in new ownership since 2011 with a young family moving in who have worked diligently over the last few years to upgrade and repair Traboyack and its grounds and this beautiful house has once again been restored to its former glory.

Entrance hall.

Dining room.

Master bedroom.

100 YEARS OF FINANCIAL STEWARDSHIP

The Watson male family line grandfather, father and son were financial custodians of Straiton St. Cuthbert's Church funds over an unbroken 100 years of service and stewardship.

First in line was William Watson, who served as church treasurer from 1906 to 1936 and was ordained as an elder on 3rd September 1911. He founded the family business, William Watson and Sons (now Straiton Stores) in 1890. Straiton Stores is now community owned and is located next door to the original shop.

Next was John Watson who succeeded his father towards the end of 1936 and was officially confirmed as church treasurer at a Kirk Session meeting in January 1937, remaining in that office until 1970. John Watson was ordained to the Kirk Session on 13th April 1941.

Finally, John Duncan Watson, son of John and grandson of William was ordained on 1st March 1970 and appointed church treasurer on the same date. He has served the church faithfully as treasurer for 36 years and at the time of writing he has also served as an elder for 49 years.

Duncan continues to be an active member of the Kirk Session, a leader and example to us all. He presently resides in Ayr with Nessie, his wife of more than 60 years.

Linkage of the Charges of
Kirmichael Parish Church with
Straiton St. Cuthbert's Parish Church

On 1st January 1971 the separate congregations agreed to enter into a linkage in terms of the draft agreement presented by the Presbytery of Ayr and approved by the General Trustees of the Church of Scotland. The document was signed on 13th February 1971 on behalf of all parties with an effective date of 31st March 1971 and consequently sharing in linkage a minister from that effective date. However, as he was due to retire the Reverend John Foster McCallum, M.A. continued at Straiton until his retiral at the end of June 1971. Kirkmichael was served by the Rev. George Dryburgh on a terminable appointment until a new minister was confirmed for the linkage. Reverend Walter D.M. Moffat accepted and confirmed to the call and subsequently was inducted on 8th July 1971 as the first minister of the Linked Charge of Kirkcmichael with Straiton. Within the terms of the linkage Reverend McCallum stayed on in The New Straiton Manse (built in 1954, when the former manse, now 'Traboyack' was put on the market) and Reverend Moffat took up residence in Kirkmichael Manse.

At a Kirk Session meeting held at "Palmullan", the home of Mr. & Mrs. McWhirter, the Moderator Reverend Moffat presented his eulogy to Reverend John F. McCallum who had passed away on 16th January 1984. It was agreed at that meeting that the Straiton Manse be kept until a new minister was appointed as Straiton was a new manse and concern had been expressed with the condition of the old manse at Kirkmichael. In the meantime, Messrs Watson and Findlay, elders would attend to the heating and security of the manse.

On 29th May 1984 a special meeting of the Kirk Session took place at Kirkmichael Manse attended by a representative of the General Trustees, that in accordance with the linkage agreement once both manses became available then in consultation with the minister and both his Sessions they had the right to select which one would be the manse of the linked charge, the other being sold.

However, this was overruled, as it had been discovered that the General Assembly had ruled and adhered to the ruling that a manse must have seven rooms and the Straiton Manse had only six. Therefore the Straiton Manse was to be sold, with the Kirkmichael manse remaining as the manse of the linkage. The matter was referred to a panel of arbiters who found in favour of the ruling. Straiton Manse was sold in October 1984 to Mr. and Mrs. James Blackwood. The Reverend W.D.M. Moffat continued to stay in the manse until he announced that he had decided to retire (citing old age) at the end of May 1985.

An Interim Moderator was appointed, the Reverend I.U. Macdonald, and so began the search that would finally end with the call to Straiton of our current minister Reverend Gerald Jones, following in the footsteps of his great grandparents who had lived and worked at Blairquhan.

The old manse was sold and on 23rd January 1990 the Kirk Sessions agreed to instruct Faulds & Sons, Maybole to proceed at once on the building of the new manse in Kirkmichael. It was dedicated at a joint service on Sunday 2nd June 1991 at 3pm by the Very Reverend Professor Robin Barbour, Dean of the Chapel Royal in Scotland.

Kirkmichael Parish Church

THE RESTORATION OF 2018–2019

Background

The church is an important landmark in the village and has a prominent position in the landscape. The building and its churchyard (both A listed), have a long ecclesiastical history and contain several graves and tombs of historic interest, including a Kennedy family tomb located in the chantry chapel, Covenanter grave and a memorial plaque for those who served in the world wars.

The church has existed since the early 13th century. The south transept of the original church, was converted and dedicated as a chantry chapel in 1475. The church was upgraded and rebuilt in 1758 and then extensively remodelled in 1901 by John Kinross. Straiton Parish Church is, along with the castles of Blairquhan and Doon, one of the most important historic buildings of the area.

Major conservation works and fabric restoration, commenced in April 2018 and now nearing completion, will ensure that the church will be maintained and preserved for use by future generations. The restoration story began almost eight long years ago and at the time of writing it seems that the time has flashed by as we near the end (well almost) of this major project. The Kirk Session (charity trustees) had been monitoring the condition of the external harling, stonework and roofing of the church, noting a marked increase in bossed and eroded areas, exhibiting signs of water penetration on all external surfaces, loss of slates and decayed leadwork. There were also significant concerns about the timber roof structure with its ageing lead and slates. An independent condition survey was commissioned by the Session in 2011. A further survey was carried out by conservation architects ARPL of Ayr in 2013 and updated by them in 2016, all of which highlighted those issues relating to roof covering decay and problems with the harled stonework. Dampness was also affecting the church interior and more especially in the oldest part, the south transept, part of the original 13th century church, where water penetration was causing damage to its interior plaster finishes. It was clear that the building was at risk of serious deterioration if the water penetration problems were not addressed.

Although some ongoing urgent repairs were being carried out, particularly on all the exposed external stonework and stained-glass windows, our planned repairs had been stretching church funds. The Session decided it was necessary to raise sufficient funds for a comprehensive repair programme to prevent the decay of the historic and valuable fabric of our A listed building. In addition to the main external and internal fabric repairs we wished to improve the environment of the interior making the church more useable and flexible for activities, with upgrading of the existing heating and lighting, and believed it would be good timing to incorporate this into a bigger project of full restoration. Included in the project we were also wishing to raising awareness of the historic and heritage value of the church both within the village community and its wider environs. As a small church within a rural village community, our financial resources were at their limit and, concerned that further deterioration would make the building less useable, we wished to halt the process of decline to ensure a sound future for the building.

As part of the development stage detailed investigations were commissioned with specialists, such as historic mortar and render analysis, bat research and timber structure decay assessments. Each of these reports were positive to the project and satisfied the criteria required to proceed with our funding applications. Development of specifications and drawings for suitable conservation repair were then developed by our conservation accredited architect. A full tender package was produced, approved by our potential funders and circulated so that we could assess the full cost of the project and prepare submissions to approvers and funders.

The necessary ecclesiastical and statutory permissions, including listed building consent, were sought and granted, allowing a full application to be submitted to the Heritage (Lottery) Fund and Historic Environment Scotland. Our applications were successful and permission to start was received on 5th February 2018.

The project was therefore fully funded, underwritten by our own fabric reserve funds together with restricted use funds held by the General Trustees on behalf of the congregation.

The Kirk Session acknowledges the assistance received from Ayr Presbytery, the Church of Scotland General Trustees and staff at Church of Scotland offices 121 George Street, Edinburgh, in moving forward with our application submission. We also acknowledge the first-class advice and assistance of the staff at the Heritage Fund (HF) which was invaluable throughout. Historic Environment Scotland (HES) matched HF funding.

Evaluation and Progress

Approved Purposes

- To undertake urgent roof and fabric repairs in to make the church building structurally sound and weathertight.
- To undertake activities including historical research by volunteers, development of heritage themed leaflets and creation of a dedicated website.
- To acknowledge the Heritage (Lottery) Fund on site, online and on all published materials.

A meeting of the community was called to present and explain our plans and funding process. An excellent turnout presented a very supportive mood to our efforts. It was explained to the meeting that, as was indicated from surveys carried out in 2011, 2013 and 2016, there had been a significant deterioration in the condition of our building and that this was now becoming a major undertaking.

- Erection of scaffolding and set-up
- Asbestos and dilapidation surveys
- Roofing and slate repairs, repair all pointing (including bell tower) to be fully determined when roof is opened to check timber supports.
- Remove and renew guttering, replace downpipes where necessary.
- Strip and renew external harling
- Repairs to windows – wood and stonework
- Address areas of water ingress – replace or repair
- Replace doors
- Strip plaster in chantry chapel
- Plaster chantry chapel
- Address areas of bubbling and decay in the main church and vestry
- Electrical – additional lighting and rewiring where necessary
- Mechanical – improve heating system plus additional radiators.

So it was with some trepidation that we saw the scaffolding arise around the church on 19th April 2018.

The initial works were carried out without any major delay and as the roof tiles were stripped it became clear that the timbers in the roof were in better condition than was feared, which was good news. The main contractors, DM Roofing were able to save a significant number of the old tiles for re-use.

The first delay occurred when on inspection of the bell tower it was discovered that the stem holding the weathervane was severely corroded and had to be replaced. A specialist blacksmith was sourced and with the removal to an external workshop for full repair, replacement and restoration the work on the roofing was held up for four weeks.

This was the first of many hold-ups (either weather-related or sub-contractors not following instruction and having to rework areas that we had thought completed). Nobody involved in the project had anticipated that it would take so long and with so many delays completion kept creeping further and further away. This certainly caused major unrest and frustration for all concerned parties.

As the general works progressed it was realised that although we had a ramp for wheelchair access at the main entrance to the church on the west gable and in 2011 had created an area for wheelchairs inside the nave, access on the approach path was proving difficult to navigate. The installation of fixings for the ramp at the front door, with adjustments and repairs to the front step had been carried out by Hubert Thomson from Kirkmichael, some years prior, who supplied all the materials as well as his own time as a gift to the church. The removal and readjustments of pews to provide the internal wheelchair area was completed by a local joiner, Peter Holden, again who gave generously of his time. After discussions with architects and the main contractor and seeking permission from South Ayrshire Council, a proposal for a disabled access path and costs was prepared and presented to HF as an addition to the Approved Purposes. HF confirmed this addition to the schedule of works to be completed.

Throughout the long process we have had regular site meetings attended by representatives from the main contractors, architects, quantity surveyors and the church; even our minister Rev. Gerald Jones attended some meetings. Thankfully the major part of the external works has been completed and we are almost at closure with the interior. The church will once again take pride of place in the community. As one of our villagers remarked, "our lovely Wee Kirk is back".

Our secondary aim was to increase visitors. Already we have shown signs that the congregation is returning, with a small increase on our regular attendance numbers prior to the restoration. Recently a party of 36 visitors from Ayrshire, the north of Scotland and Northern Ireland, were welcomed to our regular Sunday service by the Reverend Gerald Jones. They were relatives and friends gathered together to commemorate a lady who had passed away the previous year and wished to pay tribute to her by visiting Straiton Church which she had often attended.

The Chantry Chapel

The walls of the ancient chantry chapel are taking much longer than anticipated to dry out and on the advice of the plasterer the work has been delayed. Supplies of plaster and associated materials to complete this work are being stored securely on a local farm. The latest update is that the chapel walls are showing positive signs of accelerated drying and work should be able to resume soon. Discussions are under way with the contractors involved to achieve a final finish which will fulfil the wishes of most of our congregation and the majority of visitors.

As an indication of how much dampness was in the old walls of the chapel, when the existing plaster was being removed a small shrub was discovered growing inside a cavity in the east wall. With no light it was colourless, but it was getting enough moisture to survive.

"Someone may plan his journey by his own wit; but it is the Lord who guides his steps"

New English Bible: Proverbs Ch 16 V9

The Words of John Foster McCallum on the 1901 Restoration of the Nave

"So, it was that, as a result of the love and care of fine workmanship and skilled craftsmanship, a severely plain eighteenth century Presbyterian place of worship was gloriously transformed, overnight as it were, which ever since has been the admiration and the wonder of all who have come within its walls". "a thing of beauty is a joy for ever"

His words were as true today as then and were in our minds throughout the project.

Old Belfry and Church Bell

The old belfry with its ancient bell, dating back to at least the 1758 restoration, is still perched atop the apex of the nave on the west gable. It will be noted from this old drawing from 1890 (also David Cassel's earlier charcoal etching of 1889) that the bell was rung by means of a rope hanging down on the exterior face of the gable, attached to a chain on the bell mechanism in the tower. This chain can just be seen on the right of the bell in the photograph below.

Historically speaking this bronze artefact had summoned villagers to worship until superceded by a heavier apparatus in 1901, after which it was rung each Sunday morning at 9.00 am to waken the parishioners, a practice discontinued as recently as 1971. Restoration work was completed in February 1987, with the crowning of the west gable by a sturdy compartment fashioned from Northumbrian sandstone, and consistent with the contours of its ill-fated predecessor. This work was carefully carried out by Mr. John Mabon, a stonemason from Sorn.

The belfry was also further repaired and secured during the recent restoration project undertaken in 2018-2019. In December 1985 the Kirk Session resolved to proceed with the erection of a new chamber to accommodate the original bell of the 18th century church, the previous structure having been dismantled in the early 1980s for reasons of safety. The work was completed, and the belfry and bell restored *in situ* during January 1987. At the Kirk Session meeting of 23rd February 1987 it was agreed that the bell should be rededicated to the glory of God on Sunday 22nd March 1987, at a special diet of worship, with the senior elder appointed to honour this ancient instrument with its first volley of chimes in many years.

These were the Reverend W. Gerald Jones's words of the Dedication at that service: "In the faith of our Lord Jesus Christ, King and Head of the Church, Shepherd of the sheep and Guardian of lost souls, we do most solemnly dedicate once again this ancient bell, and declare it to be set apart for ever from all common and irreverent uses, and consecrated only to the honour and praise of Almighty God"

The beautiful prayer, offered by Rev. Jones at the conclusion of that dedication service, is very relevant to our present situation as we work towards the completion of the restoration project.

"Eternal God, most blessed and most holy, whom the highest heavens cannot contain, far less this house built with human hands, yet who art great and greatly to be praised: we give thee thanks for the beauty of this temple; for the furnishings with which it is adorned; for the stained glass windows which reveal to us the mysteries of light; for the melody of organ which directs us in the ministry of music; for lectern, table and pulpit which increase within us knowledge of the truth; and for the symphony and song of bells which call us weekly to thy worship.

Be present with us now, good Lord, as we hallow this instrument in thy name; that those who hear its chimes may speedily answer its call, and seek their seat within this sacred place, wherein thine honour dwells; through Him who is the sure foundation, Jesus Christ our Saviour.

Amen"

STRAITON VILLAGE AND PARISH

Straiton is a beautiful conservation village situated at the foothills of the Galloway Forest Park, in a valley through which runs the Water of Girvan. The river has its source in a small loch called the Girvan Eye, situated at a height of 1,500ft, and passes down through Straiton and Blairquhan Estate, entering the sea at Girvan.

The road to Straiton, from Ayr and North Ayrshire is via the A77 through Minishant and then turning left at 'Hoggs Corner' onto a winding country road which, to the uninitiated, seems to be much longer than the eight miles indicated on the signpost. My first visit to Straiton, accompanied by Agnes my wife, was to view a property in Fowlers Croft, almost 33 years ago. The drive was an experience; it seemed that, after going through the lovely neighbouring village of Kirkmichael, we were never going to reach our destination. Each succeeding corner rounded to superb views of farms, forests, fields, hills and castles yet did not reveal any gathering of the dwelling places that would make up a village, however small. Our first view of human habitation was glimpsed as we passed a very solidly constructed and harled bus shelter on the right, at the entrance to Milton, and then, at last, a sign announcing "Straiton". Roofs, chimneys and a church steeple came into view just beyond some old farm buildings on the left (now Craigbrae Court). It can only be said that, on entering Straiton, after the winding climbing drive up to the village, it was worth the wait. We immediately fell in love with the house, its location and view directly across to the church, positioned in the heart of the village, surrounded by a backdrop of hills up through the valley. My business life was based in Glasgow and Renfrew so, for 30 years I travelled daily from Straiton. I never tired of that winding drive as I turned in at Hoggs Corner and headed upwards to Straiton and loved the first views of Craigengower with its monument as I emerged from the tunnel of trees, just before Altizourie.

The village of Straiton was initially constructed in rows of neat uniform houses, based on the same plan, about 1760 by Thomas, Earl of Cassilis. These were mainly to house workers for the surrounding estates.

In the *Statistical Account* of 1792 William Crawford (assistant minister of the parish) noted that the occupation of the villagers was more varied, and included craftsmen, shoemakers, tailors, blacksmiths, shepherds and labourers, with more of the inhabitants turning to weaving.

The only local craftsman left at the time of the 1951 *Third Statistical Account* was the joiner, the blacksmith having emigrated to Canada in 1947. The "Smiddy" building still exists and today it has been converted and extended into a modern private house.

The Smithy, Straiton.

Mr. Crawford added in his 1792 account that previously there had been a significant number of people in the village involved in smuggling, until the authorities introduced some tightening up of the excise laws, which made those involved think again. He writes: "Before the late extension of the excise laws there was a considerable number of smugglers. The late regulations having increased the risk, at the same time diminished the profits, have in this place almost entirely put an end to this kind of illicit traffic". He also remarked that the village then had two inns and four ale-houses. "It were to be wished that ale only were sold in them".

The Black Bull Inn on the Main Street dates from 1766.

In the 13th century Straiton was referred to in various written documents as 'Strattin' or 'Stratoun'. Even as late as the 17th century the Communion cups were engraved "for the Church of Stratin". These variations may have derived from the Gaelic Strath meaning valley or simply by the usage of the times, where spelling tended to be more phonetic.

By the time the *Third Statistical Account* was being prepared leading up to its publication in 1951, village life had changed, and the social life of the residents had also changed considerably as noted in the following extracts:

"Straiton is a very friendly place with an old-world spirit"

'The nearest big towns are 14 miles away and even their smaller neighbors, including Patna, are remote enough not to count greatly. This has made it a self-contained community that is able to entertain itself without the usual excitements".

"There is a flourishing angling club which rents a stretch of the Girvan Water and has a waiting' list, a branch of the British Legion with 50 or 60 members, an active W.R.I. and a Woman's Guild, a gun club that has regular clay pigeon shoots, a curling club when there is ice on the pond at Blairquhan Castle, and a children's picnic committee, always ready to support any enterprises which serve to promote the well-being of the children".

"The Farmers' Society holds an annual show on the second Saturday of June, which is the occasion for a general holiday and attracts a great crowd from far and near".

"The centre of social life is the Straiton Club open to everybody over 15, which meets in the McCandlish Hall for all sorts of games and gatherings; last year it had 110 members".

"They have the co-operative spirit. When there is anything to be done everybody takes a hand".

The angling club, WRI, Church Guild, curling club and picnic committee are still thriving and active right up to the present time, with membership of the McCandlish Hall continuing with sessions of badminton, indoor bowls and whist evenings. The Straiton Agricultural Show is still organised by the Farmers Society on the second Saturday in June and attracts record numbers. The "Show Day Teas" in the McCandlish Hall, organised and supplied by the Church Guild, are a regular feature each year with the addition of a plant stall on the terrace outside the hall proving popular. That co-operative spirit expressed in the *Third Statistical Account* is still as strong today with our local community-owned shop and public toilets all organised and staffed with volunteer assistance.

It is interesting that the 1951 *Third Statistical Account* made detailed observations on the village church and village life, including morals: "The general level of conduct in the parish is high. There is no drunkenness and little gambling. Stealing is very rare: even the minister's apples are left untouched. Sex morals are good and there is less swearing than there was a generation ago'.

The wider parish at one time included part of the village of Patna which developed in the early 19th century beside the River Doon and astride the parish boundary with Dalmellington. Patna Church was established in 1837 as a chapel of ease from Straiton. In 1877 it became a parish in its own right.

Blairquhan

The *New Statistical Account* of 1837 notes: "The quantity of natural wood is a very pleasing feature in the scenery of the parish. Sir D Hunter Blair has planted extensively on his lands"

There are some fine old trees, chiefly sycamore, around the village and Blairquhan Estate. The most remarkable trees in the parish are the Dool (or Dule) trees of Blairquhan, on which the barons, in olden times, hung the culprits that were under their jurisdiction.

Blairquhan Estate and Castle is only about a mile from Straiton village. There has been a castle here since the 14th century although the existing building is of 19th century origin designed by Edinburgh architect, William Burn. When work began it was Sir Alexander Boswell, son of the famous James Boswell, who laid the foundation stone in 1821. The original 14th century castle became the property of the Kennedys, a branch of the family of Cassillis. In the reign of Charles II, it came into the possession of the Whiteford family; and at the end of the last century it was purchased by the present family of Hunter Blair, who are maternally descended from the Kennedys, Earls of Cassillis.

According to the Rev. Abercrombie of Maybole, it must have been a magnificent building:

> "Next to it" (Straiton), he says, "is the great Castle of Blairquhan, the fyne building and huge bulk whereof, is a plain demonstration of the sometime greatness of that family; which, besyde their possessions in Carrick, had large territories in Galloway. It is well provyded with wood, covered with planting of barren timber, and surrounded with large orchards."

Only some of the windows and mouldings from the Old Castle of Blairquhan were preserved in the kitchen court of the new castellated mansion built by Sir David Hunter Blair, Bart. (the 3rd Baronet 1800-1857). The first Baronet of Dunskey was his grandfather, Sir James Hunter Blair, who was created a baronet in 1786 and died in 1787, at Harrogate, being succeeded by Sir David's father, Sir John Hunter Blair.

The new Blairquhan Castle was finished in the year 1824. It sits upon the banks of the Girvan Water, almost exactly over the site of the ancient castle.

The grounds have been well planned and laid out with the old wood surrounding the castellated mansion adding to its striking beauty, particularly a dark avenue of lime trees that lead the visitor up to it.

During the persecution, or Killing Times as they became known, a garrison was stationed in Blairquhan, of 100 foot, and 20 horse. This was the garrison believed to be led by Lieutenant Bruce. At that time four persons were shot in the parish, of whom one, Thomas Mc'Haffie, has a tombstone erected to his memory in the churchyard.

The castle is no longer in the ownership of the Hunter Blair Family as it was sold in 2012 to its present Chinese owners, a corporate body who now run the castle as a wedding venue.

Sir Patrick Hunter Blair, 9th Baronet of Dunskey, who succeeded to the title in 2006, moved his family from Ireland to take over Blairquhan. He has now moved into the spacious Dower House and its apartments at Milton and among other appointments manages part of the retained estate.

Hills and Monuments

The hills that surround Straiton, which are numerous, rise to a considerable height. Craigengower Hill, (in Gaelic 'Hill of the goats'), in the immediate vicinity of the village, rises to the height of 1,300 feet, and Bennan Hill (Beinan, the little mountain) is about 1,150 feet high. It is where, according to the 1837 *Statistical Account* "a small obelisk was built more than half a century ago". This would date the building of the obelisk to at least before 1787. I have walked over Bennan

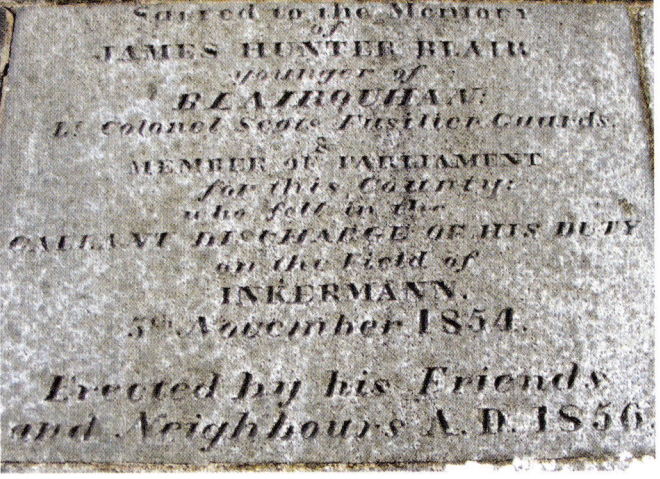

many times and have not spotted this obelisk and can only surmise that it has been removed at some point in the last 170 years or so since the Reverend Paton noted its presence.

The prominent monument, high on a hill above the village, is to Col. James Hunter-Blair, Scots Guards, who was killed at the battle of Inkerman on 5th November 1854, during the Crimean War. This monument was erected by his friends and neighbours in 1856.

On a clear day there are super views from both these hills, of Ayrshire, the Firth of Clyde, Arran, Ailsa Craig and part of the coast of Ireland.

On the summit of Bennan Hill, more than half a century ago, two carved urns, filled with ashes, were dug up. There are no Roman remains in the immediate vicinity, so they were in all probability relics of the original inhabitants of the area in pre-Roman times, although this has not been confirmed.

The local hills of Straiton, especially Craigengower have become part of the popular village paths and treks, attracting numerous ramblers and groups to the village and parish. Craigengower rises immediately behind the former manse in Straiton and is visible from all approaches to the village. Bennan Hill which is half a mile south of the village is also on a trail.

Antiquities

In the *New Statistical Account* of 1837 Robert Paton, minister at Straiton, writes "The most remarkable object of antiquity in the parish is the ruinous castle of Loch Doon, situated on an island near the head of Loch Doon". It was in ancient times a royal castle under the keeping of the Earls of Cassillis".

There is a plaque on the external eastern gable of the church confirming that several members of the Keirs family of Doon Castle were interred in the old graveyard at Straiton between 1712 and 1796.

South-west of Straiton, on Glenalla Fell, there are interesting relics of a most ancient community. Eighteen Stone Age turf houses, two hut circles and a turf dyke eight feet high are still visible. For more detailed accounts of the Antiquities of Straiton Parish and its topography it is recommended that the following be studied: The three *Statistical Accounts of Scotland* relating to Straiton Parish and Ayrshire were produced in 1792, 1837 and 1951. The first two were by Straiton ministers Rev. William Crawford in (1792) and Rev. Robert Paton (1837). The Ayrshire volume of the *Third Statistical Account of Scotland*, published in 1951, was compiled by John Strawthorn, M.A., Ph.D., Survey Officer and William Boyd, M.A., B.Sc., D.Phil, D. Litt, LL.D., Associate Survey Officer.

Evidence for a Kirkton at Straiton

Monitoring work conducted by David Swan of HS Archaeology during construction of two new houses at Straiton, South Ayrshire, identified the remains of a building that could represent evidence for an early settlement associated with the nearby church (a Kirkton). The plot under development is located immediately to the north of Straiton Parish Church, though separated by the line of the modern road.

Structure extending below modern road.

Although the nave of the present church, partially destroyed by the zealots of the Reformation, was rebuilt in 1758, its fabric contains a medieval aisle of 13th or 14th century date, and a church is mentioned in relation to this site as far back as the early 13th century, when the grant of Straiton Church to Paisley Abbey by Duncan, Earl of Carrick, was confirmed by Florence, Bishop-elect of Glasgow (1202–06).

Churches in the medieval period often acted as nuclei for the development of related settlements, and this appears to have been the case at Straiton. The church was depicted on Roy's Military Survey of Scotland, conducted in the period 1747–1755, immediately prior to the erection of the current structure, on which it was annotated as 'Kirk of Straton'. What appear to be buildings and enclosures were shown by Roy immediately to the north of the church, suggesting that there was occupation in this area before the mid-18th century. By the time of the 1st edition Ordnance Survey map of the mid-19th century, however, the plot was depicted as being largely unoccupied, and this situation remained on subsequent OS maps.

During monitoring of the initial reduction of ground level associated with the development, however, HS Archaeology identified what appears to be a clay-bonded wall foundation with a possible threshold and an associated stone floor, all of which extend below the line of the modern pavement. This, combined with cartographic evidence, suggests that the structure could represent part of the settlement shown by Roy in the mid-18th century, or could be associated with even earlier occupation associated with the church.

STRAITON (ST. CUTHBERT'S) PARISH CHURCH

Dedication Service and Exhibition 13th June 1993
& Open Day for Millennium Project 10th June 2000

STRAITON in STITCHES.

an exhibition of the new tapestry cushions for St. Cuthbert's Church, Straiton.

donation guide £1.

Foreword to the 1993 Exhibition and Service

In the *Church Service Society Annual* of 1955, the Very Revd. Dr. Ronald Selby Wright, Minister-Emeritus of the Canongate Church, Edinburgh, asks why our churches should almost be as "funereal as the ministers", noting that there is no particular sacredness in black or brown, "two of the dullest and most depressing colours". Naturally, we trust that his remarks have never been applicable to Straiton! Nevertheless, the point he wishes to make is this: that in the House of Worship, only the best is worthy of God – not only the best in words and actions, but the best in beauty, art and design.

Very recently, the Very Revd. Dr. Hugh R. Wyllie made a similar point on a visit to the Glasgow School of Art. There, he expressed his great pleasure that the Church is once again increasingly becoming a patron of the Arts, a role she had fulfilled both before and after the Reformation. In this respect, he referred to the need to enrich the Church with something meaningful and uplifting for worship – especially in the form of artistic expression and design.

With these thoughts in mind, I heartily commend to you our new chair cushions, not only as a valuable exercise, but as a means of enriching our lovely old church in Straiton in a uniquely special way, so that the beauty of the sanctuary has a simple, clear and purposeful role in our worship of Almighty God.

Throughout its history, Straiton St. Cuthbert's Parish Church has been blessed with a roll-call of kindly benefactors, each of whom, in their own way, has sought to express in wood, stone, lime and other materials something of the faith by which they lived, and for which they will ever be remembered.

Those who have made this project possible have given both to our own day, and to generations yet unborn, something of the glory of God expressed in imaginative and colourful, yet meaningful artistic form.

I would like to take this opportunity of thanking most sincerely Mary Jack and Janet Russell for their unfailing enthusiasm for this project, and not least for making the necessary arrangements to see it through from its inception to its completion. As a Kirk Session, we are very much indebted to those who kindly shared their embroidery skills over the winter months of 1992–1993, and not least to those many people of both congregation and community who have generously funded this venture.

As we now admire these works of art, knowing that we pass them on to our own successors in the faith, let our prayer be such that each will continue to nourish and enrich our worship of Almighty God in the days ahead, and in the years to come: to whom be all honour and glory, dominion and praise, now and for ever.

W. Gerald Jones
Minister at Straiton

Sunday 13th June 1993
The Prayer of Dedication:

Almighty God, our heavenly Father, greatly to be praised, and worthy of all praise: we give thanks for your abiding love by which all things are sanctified and made perfect.

Especially this day we give thanks for these furnishings, these works of tapestry and art – created for, and given to your Church – to enrich its beauty and to show forth the honour of your Name. Lord, as we now dedicate these cushions, so may the beauty of the Lord our God be upon us.

May this work, and all the symbols thereon, reflect the faith, hope and love of this community, as here again we offer and present to you ourselves, our souls and bodies, to be a reasonable, holy and living sacrifice, acceptable to you, our God and King, the Lord and Creator of all things; through Jesus Christ our Saviour.

AMEN.

"Praise God from whom all blessings flow; Praise Him all creatures here below; Praise Him above, ye heavenly host; Praise Father, Son, and Holy Ghost.

AMEN".

The Tapestry Cushions: A short commentary

This cushion project began with the objective of bringing more colour into the church. We already have two beautifully embroidered pictures on the walls: one, by Nan Walker, is a version in tapestry of Leonardo da Vinci's *The Last Supper*, and the other, also a memorial gift, was recently sewn and presented by Joan McCallum in memory of her husband.

Virtually the only other source of colour in the building is the stained glass. That formed our starting point. The principal colours in the windows are blues and yellows, while the Communion Table cover, and bookmarks are blue and gold: thus, the background colours had, so to speak, been chosen for us.

Moderator and Elders' Chairs

Three cushions for the central chairs in front of the pulpit were started as a 'pilot scheme', mainly using these colours and having their designs based on the wood-carving on the pulpit and chairs themselves, some of which were carved by a local craftsman.

The cushion on the Moderator's chair is by Mary Jack and has a border of vine leaves as on the pulpit. The chairs on either side have the emblems of the thistle and the rose carved on the backs: hence these two emblems were used by Janet Russell for these two cushions.

Moderators Chair Cushion –
by Mary Jack

Thistle Motif – by Janet Russell

Rose Motif – by Janet Russell

Choir Stalls to the right of the Pulpit

Continuing the stained-glass theme for the six choir stalls, a basic design of light shining through bars of very dark blue was decided upon, with a mid-blue panel slightly off-centre, on which various symbols, some religious and others pertaining to the local environment, could be portrayed. These cushions, when fitted in place, form a continuous line of thought – yet each has its own distinctive character.

The Lamb – by Flora Mullen

The subject of one of the stained-glass windows is Feed My Sheep. It seems particularly appropriate that the Church of St. Cuthbert here in Straiton should commemorate the saint who, according to legend, was once a shepherd boy.

The Firmament – by Ann Blackwood

The subject of the other stained-glass window is The Light of the World, which seems not unconnected with our choice of subject for the second design. This is taken from the Book of Genesis, which describes the creation of the greater and lesser lights, and "the stars also".

Praise the Lord – by Betty Lapsley

The many references in the Book of Psalms to the joy of praising God, with singing and musical instruments, suggested the harp as a motif for the third cushion, together with the bells which ring out for us each Sunday.

Choir Stalls to the right of the Pulpit

The Church of St. Cuthbert's, Straiton – by Joan McCallum

This cushion has a familiar view of a well-known landmark and much-loved building in our village.

Harvest Home –
by Shoniad Kay and Myra Paterson

No depiction of an agricultural community would be complete without reference to the fruits of their labours: hence the design of the sheaf of barley, together with some of the flora and fauna of the "corn rigs and barley rigs".

Nature Study – by Doreen McLean

The final cushion of the six shows a little of the local environment, with a few of its inhabitants, for example the forestry with the barn owl and the river and burns haunted by the heron and the dipper. No sooner had we started on the project when more volunteers came forward, and we were able to proceed to make cushions for the three remaining chairs at the baptismal font. Once again, the designs for these featured the carving already on them.

Chairs at the Priest's Door in front of the Baptismal Font in the Chantry Chapel

The Burning Bush – by Melanie Dalton.

The emblem of the Church of Scotland.

The Dove – by Morag Walker.

Symbolising the Holy Spirit descending.

The Fish – also by Melanie Dalton.

The last of the chairs has the letters carved upon it, often taken as an abbreviation of various Latin words signifying Jesus, the Redeemer. For example, among others, the letters are been held to refer to Iesus Hominum Salvator – "Jesus, Saviour of mankind". The characters of this monogram were sewn on the four corners of the cushion, but to make a more interesting centre design we used the fish, which was a secret symbol of early Christians.

Flowers and artefacts have been kindly and generously supplied by ladies of the congregation and arranged under the guidance of Myra Paterson.

Art Adviser: Mary Jack
Project Organisers: Moira Drysdale
                          Janet Russell

The organisers would like to thank all the workers for giving so much of their time and enthusiasm to the task. The results are a great tribute to their perseverance, and our reward has not only been the cushions themselves but the helpfulness and friendship we have found in each other. We are also most grateful for the interest and forbearance of families and friends in what has been both exacting and time-consuming work. In this connection, it is a heartening thought that, in several cases, daughters and even grand-daughters have added a few stitches to the work as a gesture to the future of their church.

Our thanks also to our sponsors – the workers themselves and their families who generously supported the project, and to many friends in the congregation who, while unable to assist with the actual sewing, also took part by their willingness to fund the work. Last but not least, we thank our minister and Mrs. Jones for their kind interest in our activities.

Notes on Pulpit and Chair Carvings

1. According to the Rev. John F McCallum's *Straiton Kirk* (1975), the beautiful carved oak pulpit is of Dutch design, and the gift of Mr. Alan Fergusson, Kilkerran, in memory of his sister. It is not known who gave the Communion Table, the Moderator's chair, or the choir stalls (elders' stalls).

2. The two memorial chairs on either side of the Moderator's chair (1946) were given for use at the Communion Table by the Revd. J F McCallum and his sisters in memory of their parents.

3. The three chairs in the baptistry (1965) were the gift of the Revd. J F McCallum in memory of his sister, Kate.

Straiton (St. Cuthbert's) Parish Church

Tour Guide
Open Day 10th June 2000

When you enter the church by the west door, there hangs on your right a portrayal of *The Last Supper* after Leonardo da Vinci's famous painting. This was the first contribution by an embroiderer in the village to the beautifying of the church. It was worked by Mrs. Nan Walker with her usual meticulous care.

Nearby, is a sampler commemorating the dedication in 1993 of a set of cushions for the elders' stalls. Each member of the group who made a cushion worked on the sampler in turn a copy of her own design in miniature: thus, in a way, putting her signature to her work. The change-over from the large tapestry stitches to such a small scale was quite a challenge.

Now, proceeding to the chancel, we see the real set of cushions, our original project and pioneer effort.

The 12 Tapestry Cushions in St Cuthbert's Church, Stratton were sewn by ladies of the village and sponsored by their families and friends. Dedicated on 13th June 1993.

The Original 1993 Cushions completed and ready for delivery to the Church

The three central chairs have designs based on the wood-carving on the pulpit – the vine worked by Mary Jack, and the thistle and rose by Janet Russell. The elders' cushions have a continuous design – a ribbon of light shining through bars, with a dark blue panel, each with its particular subject.

The three on the left are 'The Creation', 'The Lamb', and a familiar view of the church itself. These were made by Ann Blackwood, Flora Mullen and Joan McCallum respectively. On the right are 'Harvest Home', 'Praise the Lord' and 'Nature Study, Straiton', by Shoniad Kay, Betty Lapsley and Doreen McLean.

For those interested in the practical side of things, the canvas was double mesh, and the wool from The Weaver's Shop of the Wilton Carpet factory near Salisbury. This ensured a firm hard-wearing fabric.

Walk towards the east door and you can see on your right a tribute sewn by Joan McCallum to her late husband Malcolm McCallum [1920–1990].

Joan was a former postmistress in Straiton, and when she and her husband retired to Spain, the design and materials for her cushion were sent out to her, so that she could still take part in this work.

The Millennium Project starts on the other side of the east door with the year of 'Faith' 1997, as directed by the Church of Scotland.

Designed like a circular window to complement the 18th century style of the main part of the church, the panel represents three tenets of the Faith: The Nativity, Easter and Pentecost – as you can see from the emblems in the large circles. The smaller circles with their Celtic knots are a reminder that 1997 was the 1400th anniversary of the death of St. Columba, who brought the Christian Faith to Scotland about AD565.

On the opposite wall, at the other end of the church, is a matching circular panel. 1998 was designated by the church as the year of 'Hope'. In 'Faith' we depict past events in the Bible story. In 'Hope' we are determined to look forward with a more modern approach both as to design and subject.

The circles echo the previous year's work to some extent, but within the circles stylised figures represent individual present-day families, each with their aspirations to a better future. Together, as a community, all stretch out towards the brightness of the light from the Cross. The environment is represented by the flowers, birds and other small creatures, all attracted to the life-giving light. The technique in both panels is mainly appliqué work on a blue damask background.

Back to canvas work and to the old chapel of the church. Between the laird's door and the font are three more cushions, each using the design carved on the back of the chair: The dove, the Burning Bush and the fish. The fish was one of the secret symbols of the early Church, as was the initials carved on the chair-back and also incorporated into the cushion design. The dove is by Morag Walker and the other two by Melanie Dalton. These cushions are made up in a softer, less formal style than the others, but the same materials and colours have been used.

In keeping with the medieval origin of the chapel there are two hassocks in heraldic designs, one the quartered shield of the Kennedy family who then owned land here, and for whom this chantry chapel was built. In the 18th century they also founded, in outline, the present village of Straiton. The other hassock bears the escutcheon of the present lairds, the Hunter Blair family of Blairquhan.

Beside the arch leading to the old chapel is the Millennium Banner, the climax of our three-year project, of 'Faith', 'Hope' and 'Love'. Not quite needle-point but in very fine canvas, using the finest Persian wools, this depicts the principal features of the village: the bridge over the Kirk Burn, the Main Street with the Black Bull on the right, the McCandlish Hall, the former manse, now Traboyack, the school, and Blairquhan Castle. The church has pride of place in the centre. This is not a photographic reproduction of the village, but it is more an 'impression' of the familiar buildings and features of it. From the clouds above Craigengower and the monument, silver trumpets proclaim the Good-News message of

'Faith', 'Hope' and 'Love', while in the darkened sky can be seen the Dove of Peace and of the Holy Spirit, as well as the eclipse of the sun, and finally the Star of Bethlehem. The stand was made from a disused pew and finished to match the rest of the church woodwork. The banner is lined with crimson silk, the initials of all the workers being embroidered on the back.

The volunteers from the congregation and community who worked on this project were: Ann Blackwood, Mary Jack, Betty Lapsley, Doreen McLean, Flora Mullen, Jane Rosie, Janet Russell and Morag Walker. Once again, our heartfelt thanks go to them for such an outstanding contribution to the "Colour" of our worship.

James McCosh
(1811–1894)

James McCosh, prominent Scottish philosopher and president of the College of New Jersey (later to become Princeton University) 1868-1888 was born at Carskeoch, Parish of Straiton, 1st April 1811, the eldest son of Andrew, a farmer from Ayr.

McCosh first enrolled at the University of Glasgow in 1824, aged 13, and studied an Arts course over five years, taking classes in Latin, Greek, Logic, Ethics, and Physics. In session 1827-1828 he was awarded a prize in the senior division of the junior class of Mathematics. In 1828-1829 he gained another prize in Natural Philosophy 'for propriety of conduct, exemplary diligence, and display of eminent ability in examinations on the subjects of lectures, Essays and investigations connected with Physical Science'. He went on to graduate MA from Edinburgh in 1833.

McCosh entered the ministry, serving as minister of Abroath from 1835 to 1839; Brechin from 1839 to 1843, and the Free Church there from 1843 to 1851. In 1851 he was awarded an LLD from Marischal College, Aberdeen, and in the same year took up the appointment as Professor of Logic and Metaphysics at Queen's College, Belfast, where he remained until 1868. In 1868 McCosh was appointed 11th President of the College of New Jersey, and Professor of Biblical Instruction and Philosophy. The College of New Jersey, which was chartered in 1746, achieved university status in 1896 and was officially renamed Princeton University. That same year 1868, he was awarded honorary degrees from the Universities of Brown (DD), Washington Jefferson (DD), and Harvard (LLD). From 1888 to 1894, McCosh was Lecturer of Philosophy at Princeton. He died there on 16th November 1894.

James McCosh
As President of the College of New Jersey (later to become Princeton University) 1868-1888

James McCosh took office exactly 100 years after his fellow Scot, John Witherspoon. When he came to Princeton he was already well-known throughout the English-speaking world as an author, philosopher, and Free Churchman. One alumnus, who had been a freshman in 1870, compared the new president's influence to "an electric shock, instantaneous, paralysing to the opposition. and stimulating to all that were not paralysed."

McCosh gathered a distinguished faculty; revised and modernized the plan of study; developed elective course options; and instituted graduate work. He founded schools of science, philosophy, and art, and he began an ambitious programme of building and planting that greatly enhanced the formerly bare campus. A strong proponent of the Greek idea of "sound body, sound mind," he included a gymnasium and a library in his building programme.

He was a teaching president, holding regular classes in the history of philosophy and in psychology and conducting seminars in *Prospect*, the new presidential mansion.

When Darwin's *Origin of Species* (1859) threatened to overturn age-old beliefs in God's creation and government of the world, McCosh stood out almost alone among American clergymen in defending evolutionary doctrine, insisting that the Darwinian hypothesis, far from denying the existence of God, served "to increase the wonder and mystery of the process of creation."

Like John Witherspoon before him, McCosh took a commonsense approach to the curriculum of the College, one that was liberal yet firm. Students were encouraged to choose a wide range of electives that were to be taken side by side with obligatory and disciplinary courses, mathematics "to solidify the reasoning powers," and Classics "to refine the taste." McCosh enriched the extracurricular life of the campus, making the "four long years" more enjoyable.

During his time, many undergraduate activities began to assume their present form. The Glee Club, the Dramatic Association (later known as the Triangle Club), and the first intercollegiate football team were formed under his benevolent gaze. And, although he disapproved mightily of secret Greek fraternities, he allowed a group of upperclassmen to form the first permanent eating club.

Throughout his life, McCosh shared credit with his wife, Isabella. "She advised and assisted me in all my work," he said. Daughter of an eminent physician, Isabella McCosh was Princeton's unofficial nurse, the one and only medical presence on the campus. Later, when the trustees built an infirmary, they named it for her.

In his parting words to the College, McCosh said, "I am reminded keenly that my days of active work are over. But I take the step firmly and decidedly. The shadows are lengthening, the day is declining. My age, seven years above the threescore and ten, compels it, providence points to it, conscience enjoins it, the good of the College demands it. I leave it with the prayer, that the blessing of Heaven and the good will of men may rest upon it, and with the prospect of it having greater usefulness in the future than even that which it has had in the past."

It is important to note that the connection with Straiton and Princeton Theological Seminary is now strengthened by the fact that our current minister of almost 34 years is a graduate of Princeton. The Right Reverend Dr. Angus Morrison MA, BD, PhD, DD, then Moderator of the Church of Scotland visited Straiton Church on Sunday 13th March 2016. After conducting the service he also visited the McCosh family grave and memorial to John McCosh. The Moderator was a visiting Scholar at the Theological Seminary from July to October 2009.

The Reverend Roderick Lawson and the Reverend James McCosh

The Reverend Roderick Lawson (1831–1907) was Parish Minister at the West Church in Maybole, or the "Glen Kirk" where he was ordained on 14th April 1863 and faithfully ministered to his parish for 34 years. He was a former teacher and had been persuaded to leave teaching and took up initial studies for the ministry at Glasgow University and later entered Edinburgh University to study divinity. There is no record of him actually graduating from Glasgow, although his transfer to Edinburgh signalled his entry into the ministry. He started off his ecclesiastical career as Assistant to Reverend John MacLeod at Newton-on-Ayr.

Reverend Lawson was very much a local man. He was born in Girvan on 15th March 1831, died at Ayr on 26th February 1907 and is buried at Maybole Cemetery. From his time in the teaching profession he had a passion for writing and continued with that through his ministerial life, being a prolific author of some 20 published books as well as several songs and poems, many of those reflecting his love of his native Ayrshire.

In his book, *Places of Interest About Girvan*, there are two very interesting parts relating to our Church of St. Cuthbert's in Straiton and his connection with the Reverend James McCosh. The first relevant part relates to his description of Straiton Church as it was at that time:

> "The Parish Church of Straiton is strangely composed of two portions. There is first the old aisle, built of hewn stone, with gothic window, and outside staircase, and then there is the modem white-washed portion, as plain and bald as may be. The old aisle formed part of the Roman Catholic Church which stood here before the Reformation and shews the stress men then laid on beauty in church architecture.
>
> The modem barn-like building, with its square windows and rough-cast walls, shews the little taste and less cost our Protestant forefathers expended on the worship of God. In this way, Straiton Church is a standing parable regarding the two forms of faith. It is true the building is now purged of its crucifixes and images, and even the stone cross which once overtopped the gable of the aisle has been demolished".

In addition, the Reverend Lawson refers to the old church graveyard (which now is also A Listed along with the church), remarking on the oldest stone within the burial ground. According to his notes the inscription was obviously clearer on his visit than it is now. In the booklet published in 1999, *Straiton Churchyard Monumental Inscriptions* transcribed and compiled by Gordon and David Killicoat, this stone numbered 154 was recorded as "Table stone – Illegible". In an updated 2009 edition, by the Alloway and Southern Ayrshire Family History Society, the stone 154 is noted as "having another stone lying on top with no inscription visible"; this is how the stones are placed at the present time.

Reverend Lawson notes: "The oldest stone, which lies immediately below the Gothic window, bears the following inscription":

> 'Here rests the bodie of Mr. John M'Quorne, younger, in hope of the joyful resurrection. He died in peace, 1st May 1612, aged 23. VIXL VIVO MELIVS. OPTIME VIV AM' "I have lived: I am living better – I shall yet live best of all".

This was believed to be the resting place of a son of the second John McQuorne, who had been minister of Straiton. However, it is noted that John Mcquorne the Elder who took over from his father in 1598 had four children James, Samuel Jean and Elizabeth. This stone is more likely to be that of James (perhaps referred to locally as John).

The second part that is most relevant to the story of Straiton and its "Wee Auld Kirk" tells the tale of a visit to Straiton by the President of Princeton University.

"In this Churchyard are also buried several generations of the M'Cosh's of Carskeoch, near Patna, whose Family tree has blossomed in these modern days into Ex-President James M'Cosh, of Princeton College, New Jersey, United States.

Some years ago, I remember having gone, by arrangement, to preach at Straiton, and found that the President was there, staying for a few days with his sister, the late Mrs. M'Adam, of Dalmorton. He came into the vestry that morning, and asked leave to preach for me, as it was the last opportunity, he thought, he should have of preaching in the church of his boyhood. I, of course, consented, and he chose as the subject of his remarks those verses in the 16th chapter of John, which set forth the office and work of the Holy Spirit.

At the conclusion, he spoke a few words about his early connection with Straiton Church and pointed out the pew in which he used to sit. In those days, he said, the whole family was in the habit of walking every Sunday to church across the moor (4 miles) and returning after service. All the young lads of his own age whom he knew at that time were now dead, many of them having wasted their lives through strong drink.

He had thought it right to leave the Church of Scotland, and even Scotland itself; but though living in America, he had still a warm side to his native land, his native parish, and the old church round which his fathers were resting, and he was glad to have this opportunity of saying these things within its walls.

After service, I was invited to dine with the President at the Manse. He was very pleasant and affable, dwelling much on old times and persons. I asked him how he liked the Americans and mentioned that I had heard they used ministers there as they used oranges and suck all the juice out them, and then fling them away. He said it might be so in some cases, but they certainly had not so used him.

If I might judge from what I heard that day, I should say that the President could never have been a pulpit orator, although there was a certain homely earnestness about his words which had their own effect.

He had however found his life-work in training students, and writing philosophical treatise, the most popular of these being the *Method of the Divine Government*. In this way he has become a man of mark, a credit to Straiton, to Ayrshire, and to the Presbyterian Church generally.

The oldest member of the M'Cosh family buried in Straiton Churchyard is Jasper M'Cosh, who died in 1729: and I remember the old President (now in his 81st year), when he came out of the church, went to look at the stone, told me it was the oldest record of his family he could trace, said he would never see it again, and then stooped down and affectionately patted the weather-worn memorial, as he took his final leave of it".

McCandlish Hall

"McCandlish Hall, Straiton, opened 22nd Nov., 1912.

Completed in 1912 "The Hall" is located on the attractive scenic Main Street directly in the centre of our village. With its main hall, stage, kitchen/reading room it provides the social centre for the villagers and visitors alike.

A view of Straiton village showing the proximity of the McCandlish Hall and St. Cuthbert's Church.

The Hall was at the centre of the Coronation Celebrations for George V1 in 1937.

12th May 1937 was to be the date of the Coronation of Edward VIII who became king on 20th January 1936, on the death of his father George V, and abdicated 11th December 1936. The Coronation already planned then went ahead for George VI on that day.

Straiton Church has maintained a close association with the Hall through the years since its opening in 1912. Over that period the Hall has been the host for church activities, fundraising events and Kirk Session meetings, even standing in for the church in holding Sunday Service on occasions both planned and unplanned. Our guild also has its regular meetings in the Hall, running from October to March.

The Hall is managed by a hall committee and the minister of St. Cuthbert's Church is usually in the chair. The committee's hard-working Secretary, who has been in post for a considerable number of years, is Margaret Logan the church's Session Clerk.

The hall committee have recently been successful in raising funds themselves through various grants and public subscription towards an extension to the Hall for the provision of disabled toilets.

Church Fundraising and the Hall

As part of the church's fundraising efforts to raise funds for our restoration project two 'Auction of Promises' events, organised by Members of the Kirk Session, took place in 2012 and 2017, raising significant sums.

Our Other Regular Fundraising Events:

Annual sponsored walk round Straiton with soft drinks station and teas in the Hall.

Annual Xmas Fayre – Part of funds raised given to a charity chosen by the stallholders.

Church and John McHaffie, Covenanter

Largs Farm

In Straiton Churchyard rest the remains of Thomas McHaffie, a native of the parish, who, after repeated escapes from the hands of the troopers, was at length captured and shot on the farm of Linfairn. A memorial stone, which was erected in 1824, alongside of the old one, bears the following inscription:

"Here lies Thomas McHaffie, Martyr, 1686.
Though I was sick and like to die,
Yet bloody Bruce did murder me,
Because I adhered in my station,
To our Covenanted Reformation.
My blood for vengeance yet doth call
Upon Zion's haters all."

The original stone which was to the right of the new memorial stone (on the left in the photograph) has been refurbished by Historic Environment Scotland.

Thomas McHaffie was the son of John McHaffie, farmer at Largs Farm, close to Straiton Village. McHaffie attended field preachings known as conventicles and it is probable that he would mainly attend those that were held near Maybole and as usual he would walk over the hills to these to a predetermined secret location.

The "Killing Years" ranged approximately from 1680 to 1688 and it was a dangerous time for those adherents to the National League and Covenant who wished only to maintain their right to worship in faith as they always had. They were so persecuted for that very fact and at the mercy of the might of the troopers and dragoons as they made their way to the conventicles.

Largs Farm, Straiton, Ayrshire.

These were not fanatical as Parliament had made them out to be in their pronouncement of May 1685 and were not ignorant of the fact that they continued to give the authorities opportunity to put them on trial or simply "to the sword" each time they attended a field preaching or asked to take the Oath of Abjuration after it was introduced in that year.

There are many writers and commentators on these Killing Times, and I have chosen the Reverend Dr. Robert Simpson's anecdotal tale of Thomas McHaffie taken from his book *Traditions of the Covenanters* published in 1846.

> "Thomas McHaffie, of the Parish of Straiton in Carrick was one day proceeding to a meeting near Maybole but was observed and pursued by a company of troopers, who probably had been advertised of the projected conventicle. He fled back to a very wild retreat called the Star, in the upper part of Ayrshire, where it borders on Galloway. The desolation of this region is extreme, being a territory entirely covered with rocks and stones without end. To this rugged seclusion McHaffie was joined by two of his covenanting friends".

The Rev. Simpson goes on to describe the location further explaining how they felt quite safe in Star due to its inaccessibility to horsemen and following the departure of the pursuers Thomas took out his Bible, a constant companion, and it is said that he read to his friends the words of Psalm 102.

> 'For he hath looked down from the height of his sanctuary; from heaven did the Lord behold the earth; to hear the groaning of the prisoner; to loose those that are appointed to death'.

He was listed on the Fugitive Roll published on 5th May 1684, with his two companions Allan and William Carrie, who were also listed as living at Largs Farm. McHaffie spent two years on the run after being declared a rebel in 1684 although it is noted that he had been declared a fugitive at a circuit court held at Ayr on 19th June 1683. There has been some discussion about the veracity and piousness of the Rev. Simpson's story as he does admit that it is an anecdote. However, it is based on a true story as there is no doubt that McHaffie was killed at Linfairn in 1686.

The earliest written account of the death of McHaffie was in a "Short Memorial" by Alexander Shields in 1690 only four years after the event:

> "The said Captain Bruce and his Men took out of his bed Thomas McHaffie, sick of a Feaver and shot him instantly, in the Paroch of Stratoun in Carrick, Jan 1686".

Thomas Mchaffie had continued to remain as a fugitive hiding in various caves and other places in the hills throughout Straiton Parish until fate dealt him another blow. He fell ill as he had spent most of his time in damp caves and out in the open exposed to all extremes of weather. He moved closer to home and arrived in an area close to Linfairn Farm, south of Straiton, where he made himself a rough shelter in the ground between two waterfalls.

None of the writers of the various accounts have recorded the fate of his companions at Star, Alan and William Carrie. We can only assume that they parted company at some time in the two years which had passed since their arrival at Star.

Again, I return to the Rev. Robert Simpson's slightly pious (to be expected of a minister) and anecdotal tale:

> "This good man, however, did not always so escape the vengeance of his enemies; for he ultimately fell into their hands, and obtained the martyr's crown. On the morning of the day on which he was shot, he was concealed in a glen on the farm of Linfairn, in the parish of Straiton. At this time, he was very unwell and weakly, owing to exposure in the cold damp caves in which he was forced to hide himself from his foes. In this sickly condition he heard the approach of the soldiers and rose from his resting-place to flee for his life.
>
> He reached the house of a friend, but he no sooner entered than he threw himself on a bed, being feverish and exhausted. Captain Bruce, who commanded the party, arrived at the house, and made M'Haffie an easy prey. He ordered his men to drag him from his couch, which they instantly did, and having led him out to the field, they, without ceremony, shot him dead on the spot. This murder was committed in the depth of winter 1685. A rude stone on the farm of Linfairn marks the identical spot where he fell. He was interred in the churchyard of Straiten"

The Rev. Simpson then highlights another version of the same event from a book by the Rev. Robert Wodrow in his book *The History of The Sufferings of The Church of Scotland from the Restoration to the Revolution* which records the details of McHaffie's capture and death:

> "Sometime in this month (January), Thomas M'Hassie (M'Haffie), son to John M'Hassie, in the Largs, in the parish of Straiton, in Carrick, was despatched quickly. This good man was lying in his house very ill of a fever. Captain Bruce and a party of soldiers coming into the house, put questions to him, which he refusing to answer, and declining to take the abjuration oath, they took him out of his bed to the high road nearby, and without any further process, or any crimes I can hear of laid to his charge, shot him immediately."

This account makes it clear that Captain Bruce did enter the house as well as his men to ensure the capture (or death) of the fugitive. The Rev. Simpson tends to make comment on the piety of the Covenanters and is scathing towards the "poor ignorant Dragoons and their ignorant but more barbarous Commanders."

Although he was buried in Straiton Kirkyard, where three stones mark his grave, a boulder lying in a field near to Linfairn Farm is said to mark the spot where McHaffie was executed.

In *Jardine's Book of Martyrs* by Dr. Mark Jardine there is some discussion about the Rev. Robert Simpson's anecdotes and the reality of the stone marking the spot. This type of killing happened to so many people from all over the Lowlands and Central Scotland and these tales from the Killing Times are ever present of "Man's Inhumanity to Man". Thomas McHaffie is our martyr part of Straiton folklore, and he deserves not to be forgotten.

Dr. Jardine has also provided in his written work on this subject a full and detailed account of the other main character in these events, Captain Bruce.

According to all the early sources, the officer responsible for McHaffie's execution was Captain Bruce as the 'captain of dragoons' who was responsible for many other killings of Covenanters and was extremely capable in the continued hunting down of fugitive covenanters or rebels as they were called.

Dr. Jardine informs the reader:

> "From the evidence of the registers of the privy council, it is clear that 'Captain Alexander Bruce' was the same individual as the 'Lieutenant Alexander Bruce' who served in Lieutenant-Colonel Lord Charles Murray's troop of His Majesty's Regiment of Dragoons.
>
> Lieutenant Bruce was responsible for both the killings at Lochenkit and the shooting of Kirko. At the time of those killings, Bruce held a lieutenant's commission, but he was nearly always referred to as 'Captain Bruce' in official correspondence from late 1684 onwards.
>
> Before joining the Dragoons, he had held the rank of captain in Colonel Kirkpatrick's Regiment in the Scots Brigade in the United Provinces, until, under the name of 'Captain Alexander Bruce of Broomhall', he was commissioned as a lieutenant in Murray's troop on 11th May 1683. His diligence also saved the life of James Lawson, the minister of Irongray, on 8th February 1686, Lawson wrote to the privy council commending Bruce's actions in rescuing him, bringing in prisoners and killing the Covenanters at Lochenkit.
>
> Three days later, on 11th February, the privy council rewarded Bruce by recommending to his Grace the Duke of Queensberry; Lord High Treasurer, to give Captain Alexander Bruce such 'ane allowance as his Grace shall think fitt upon the account of the good services done by him against the rebells in apprehending and bringing them in prisoners'.
>
> He was promoted to captain-lieutenant, alongside Murray's promotion to colonel, on 6nd November 1685, and awarded the rank and precedency of a captain of horse by James VII on 18th October 1688. Despite his loyal service to the restoration regime, Bruce switched sides at the Revolution. He was knighted by William of Orange and appointed Muster-Master-General of the Forces in Scotland on 22nd February 1690".

Alexander Bruce was the first son of Robert Bruce and Helene Skene Bruce. Robert Bruce was a Lord of Session as Lord Broomhall, and owner of the Broomhall estate near Dunfermline. Alexander Bruce represented the burgh of Culross in the Parliaments of 1661–1663, 1669–1673, 1678, 1685 and 1686. In 1705, he succeeded his cousin, Alexander Bruce, as the 4th Earl of Kincardine. He married his second cousin once removed, the only daughter of Robert Bruce of Blairhall. Thereafter he began to build Broomhall House in 1702 to be a lasting achievement of his career as a soldier. He died on 3rd October 1715 and was succeeded by his son Robert.

COVENANTERS

Background

The process of "Reformation" of the Church in Scotland in the 16th century was driven by two main factors. The first was the corruption within the Roman Catholic church at that time – the wealthy were often able to buy absolution for their sins and misdemeanors, with the money going to the church (or in some cases, the local clerics, some of whom did little to attend to their pastoral duties).

There was also a process of rejecting the power of the Church of Rome and adopting instead an organisation where the people had a form of worship where they felt they had a more direct communication with God. Of course, the zealots on both sides considered that they followed the only "true" religion and conflicts continued between the remaining Catholics and the adherents to the reformed church.

The situation was not helped by the continued bias of the monarch towards the Catholic Church. King Charles I in particular, preferred to be head of the church, rather than accepting the Presbyterian principles of a self-governing organisation. Charles also pursued his vision of the "Divine Right of Kings", believing that as God had appointed him king, his decisions on all matters were above question.

National Covenant

In 1637 King Charles I attempted to introduce an Episcopal "Book of Common Prayer" which was seen as an attempt to anglicise Scotland and the church. There was outrage, particularly as there was no prior discussion with the General Assembly, the governing body of the Church of Scotland. In St. Giles' Cathedral, Jenny Geddes famously hurled her folding-stool at the pulpit screeching "Daur ye say mass in my lug".

The following year, in February 1638, with high emotion, a new National Covenant was drawn up and thousands crowded into Greyfriar's Churchyard in Edinburgh to sign it. This document drew on an earlier "King's Confession" in 1581 in which a covenant had been drawn up in which both the king and the people swore to maintain the Presbyterian system of church government. While the new document swore loyalty to the monarch, it nevertheless firmly restated the direct

St. Giles' Cathedral

relationship between the people and God, with no interference from the king and "all kinds of Papistry". Within months, over 300,000 people had "covenanted" in what a writer of the day described as "the glorious marriage day of the Kingdom [of Scotland] with God". The adherents were prepared to fight for their religious freedom – and soon were called upon to do so.

Civil War and the Solemn League and Covenant

Charles advocated the suppression of Puritanism in favour of a "high" church with richness and ceremony, but it was not just for religious reasons that the conflict between King Charles I and Parliament broke out. He had dissolved Parliament in 1629 and ruled alone for eleven years.

The Puritans and the English Parliament eventually rose up against the king. Civil war broke out between the Royalists who supported the king, and the Puritans, led by an astute general, Oliver Cromwell. The English Parliament sought the support of the Scottish Parliament and army. The Scots agreed – but only after the English had undertaken to reform their church along the lines of that in Scotland. Desperate for their support, the English Parliament agreed and the "Solemn League and Covenant" was signed in 1643.

Initially, the war went in favour of the king, even in Scotland where James Graham of Claverhouse, 1st Marquess of Montrose, won a number of battles against the Covenanter forces. Montrose had initially signed the Covenant himself, but the excesses of the religious zealots convinced him to support the king instead. But by 1646 King Charles I was forced to surrender – to the Scottish Covenanter army, rather than the English forces.

Charles tried to sow dissension between the Scots and the English, but he was eventually handed over to the English Parliament. Having achieved their aims, the English ignored the religious element of the deal. Then, much to the horror of many in Scotland, King Charles I was executed in 1649. His loyal supporter in Scotland, the Marquess of Montrose, escaped to Norway but returned to Scotland in 1650. He lost a battle at Carbisdale and was betrayed by MacLeod of Assynt for £25,000 (a huge sum in those days). He was sentenced to death by the Scottish Parliament, without a trial, and was hanged.

King Charles II

Charles II then came to the Scots to appeal to their sense of loyalty to the Crown. That support was given only after he had signed the National Covenant.

He was crowned "King of Scots" at Scone in 1651 but had to escape to France as Cromwell's forces marched into Scotland. Cromwell's subjugation of the country gave rise to rebellion from those who still supported their "covenanted king". When King Charles II was restored in 1660, he turned his back on the Covenant he had signed and tried to restore Episcopacy and revoked all the legislation passed by the Scottish Parliament from 1640.

The Covenanters rebelled and left the established church and resorted to "conventicles" in the countryside, with their ministers preaching in the open air. Armed rebellion soon followed, especially in the south-west of Scotland and in Ayrshire. Between 1661 and 1688 it is estimated that 18,000 died both in battles and persecution, creating martyrs and lasting bitterness.

In 1666 at the Battle of Rullion Green in the Pentland Hills, the king's army, led by Sir Thomas Dalyell, defeated the Covenanters. John Graham of Claverhouse, who later became Viscount Dundee and a supporter of the Jacobite cause, was at the forefront of what became known as the "Killing Times".

On June 1st 1679 Claverhouse came across a conventicle of several thousand people at Drumclog. With a fighting force of around 1,500, the Covenanters outnumbered the dragoons by around four to one: the government forces were routed and chased from the field. However, a few weeks later the Duke of Monmouth subdued the Covenanters at Bothwell Bridge. Persecution continued for another nine years with the last Covenanter to be executed in February 1688.

Eventually, some degree of order was restored in 1690, with the accession of William of Orange and Queen Mary. Even so, some extreme Covenanters known as "Cameronians", who disliked William of Orange because he had not signed the Covenant, continued to object for a while.

Debate and conflict on religious matters continued to rumble on and came to a head in 1843 with the break-up of the Church of Scotland and formation of the Free Church of Scotland. But that's another story.